BROTHERS

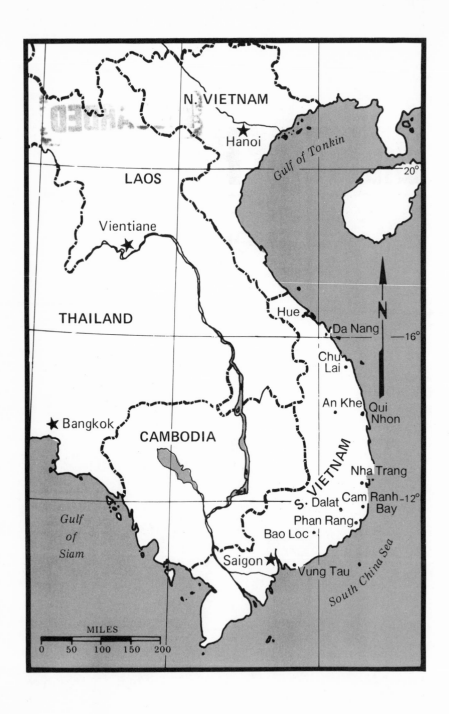

BROTHERS

Black Soldiers in the Nam

**Stanley Goff
Robert Sanders
with
Clark Smith**

PRESIDIO PRESS

ARMS & ARMOUR PRESS

Published simultaneously by Presidio Press, 31 Pamaron Way,
Novato, CA 94947 and Arms and Armour Press, 2–6 Hamp-
stead High Street, London NW3 IQQ

Library of Congress Cataloging in Publication Data

Goff, Stanley.
  Brothers, black soldiers in the Nam.

  1. Vietnamese Conflict, 1961–1975 —
Personal narratives, American. 2. Vietnamese
Conflict, 1961–1975 — Afro–Americans. 3. Goff,
Stanley. 4. Sanders, Robert. I. Sanders,
Robert. II. Smith, Clark, 1934–
III. Title.
DS559.5.G63   959.704'38   82–5244
ISBN 0–89141   139–9   AACR2

ISBN (UK) 0 85368 564 9

Book design by Vicki Martinez
Cover design by Kathleen A. Jaeger
Printed in the United States of America

CONTENTS

He who is a friend
is a friend always,
And brothers are born
for adversity.

Proverbs 17:17

1968. *At the time we were running into other companies that were at least 50 percent black. We'd meet them out in the boonies and there'd be an immediate rapport:*
   "Hey, man, what's going on?"
   "Awright, awright!"
   "Where you from?"
   "Chicago."
   "San Francisco."
   "Yeah, man? Is that right?"
   "Right on, brother."
   "What's going on, man. Hey, you guys been getting into any heavy shit?"
   "Yeah, Charlie kicked our ass about three or four days ago, man. Beware!"
   They'd be on one side of the stream; we'd be on the other side. We wouldn't stop long. The CO knew we'd start bull-shitting and having fun. So everybody's shouting:
   "Where you from? What company, man?"
   "Echo Company."
   "Yeah, we're Bravo Company!"
   Then we'd go off in opposite directions; maybe never see them again.

FOREWORD
By Clark Smith

Brothers fought the war in Vietnam—and out in the field among the infantry grunts at least half of them were black. Not since the Civil War, when inductees with money were allowed to buy their exemptions from the national draft, has the burden of military service so directly fallen on a single group of Americans. No national advantage came from a black man's fight in Southeast Asia, but black casualties in Vietnam far exceeded white casualties in proportion to black representation among Americans. Perhaps all American wars can be described as the Civil War was: "A rich man's war, a poor man's fight." But the tendency to channel blacks into the infantry, to be sent to Vietnam, to serve overlong in combat units, suggests that the war in Vietnam was too often a "white man's war, a black man's fight."

Blacks and whites fought in integrated units throughout the Vietnam War. Their home away from home was the pack on their back; they humped the most rugged terrain in the world and, during the war, certainly the most dangerous. They were sent to seek out and destroy an aggressive and resilient enemy.

But because of the firepower and air mobility of a technologically superior force, American tactics called for use of infantrymen as decoys. Instead of seizing ground and holding it as in previous wars, American troops sought to flush the enemy from concealed positions in order to destroy them with superior firepower. In response, the enemy developed the art of concealment, hiding and tunneling in the dense terrain, while fighting a hit–and–run defensive war of attrition. These conditions of war made the American infantryman more vulnerable. His offensive capabilities were used against him.

American combat units had to seek out their Vietnamese adversary in unfamiliar areas, often under oppressive conditions, and draw them into a more conventional military encounter. Each army sought to fight the war on its own terms; each claimed great success, but at even greater human cost. The single most powerful weapon of the American forces was their mobility. Provided by the multi-purpose helicopter which rapidly transported men and materiel over wide areas of Vietnam, it saved countless lives while working to destroy the enemy. The enemy's single most frightening response was use of the booby trap and the ambush, which made a dangerous and unfamiliar terrain even more hazardous. The war became a struggle over "body counts" — Vietnamese and American. For all the vast technological instrumentation by the American military, the American infantryman played a crucial tactical role. Black Americans were at the center of this military vortex of death and destruction.

For the black soldier in Vietnam there were two wars. As infantry "grunt" he confronted "Charlie" — the Vietnamese regular or irregular soldier — across the length of Vietnam. But the black soldier also confronted an older adversary: racism. Though blacks have fought in all American wars, and in the Korean War in integrated units, never before had blacks played the paramount role they did in Vietnam. So if the military service was for blacks a vehicle for social equality in which rank replaced race as a measure of respect and accomplishment, it was also a locus of institutional racism in which competence challenged prejudice. It is fair to say that the black soldier proved himself equal to the task even when events worked to his disadvantage. His struggle for respect often was made against *both* racism and rank. The record is unclear on how many of the 50 percent of black infantrymen walked point or carried the infantryman's "artillery" — the M-60 machine gun. But blacks filled these crucial slots in preponderant numbers. Their vital role is reflected in black battlefield casualties — and every grunt knows the hazards of walking point or carrying the firepower of an infantry platoon. The job of rifleman and machine gunner is not associated with civilian skills. Every Vietnam veteran understands the irony of this form of on-the-job training. But it was in the heroic service to their country that an otherwise unemployed nineteen-year-old soldier could gain respect against which accomplishments could be measured. Respect and accomplishment are the noblest adversaries of racism.

The struggle for equality is tied to war. The Gulf of Tonkin incident shared headlines with the murder of civil rights workers in Mississippi. The fracturing of the Civil Rights Movement and the murder of Martin Luther King coincided with the turning point of the Vietnam War, which King began to oppose. In eight years of tough war, perhaps the toughest year was 1967. It was the year of the largest draft calls, a year in which the public view of the war began its negative drift. The increase in combat anticipated the Tet Offensive of 1968. It was exactly at that point that Stan Goff and Bob Sanders went to war — at the halfway mark when the war had already begun to lose its purpose and resolve. But the nineteen-year-old recruits did not know that. Their attention was turned toward service and survival. This concern took its distinctive path in the Vietnam War. The rotational system devised by the military to service its manpower needs smoothly and efficiently meant that, except for the initial units sent to Vietnam, every Vietnam GI was a replacement. He went to Vietnam as an individual, most likely among strangers. Though trained in the mili-

tary skills, survival was as often a matter of luck. The historical
irony of the Vietnam experience of black veterans like Stan and
Bob was that combat efficiency and military responsibility
meant vastly increased risks. Because both Stan and Bob carried "the pig" (the M–60 machine gun), they were in positions
of great responsibility and jeopardy. They were trapped in a
tactical situation in which survival meant risk.

After four months in combat with the 196th Light Infantry
Brigade operating in southern I Corps, Stan earned the Distinguished Service Cross for bravery under fire. Bob, an airborne
trooper with the 173rd Airborne in southern II Corps, earned
the Air Medal for more than twenty–five combat assaults. Stan
emerged from Vietnam combat unscathed. Bob was slightly
wounded in his eleventh month of combat duty. They shared
with both black and white soldiers that "unity and harmony"
that promoted survival among combat units at a time when
racial incidents brought increasing disharmony to the rear
echelon. Their accounts of their personal survival are not
unique. In the dirty war in Southeast Asia, there were everyday
incidents of bravery, loyalty, and self–sacrifice that rivalled
those of arrogance, brutality, and stupidity. The brothers
understand this final irony of war.

Brothers is an attempt to give the black Vietnam veteran a
voice in the history of the Vietnam War. Too often it is forgotten that the military executors of American foreign policy
had to base their success or failure in Vietnam ultimately on the
man in the field with the weapon. And, as often as not, that man
was black. He was the "minority" executor of a Vietnam policy
which, ironically, prolonged the colonial tradition which for so
long had burdened Indo–China. Though this development was
not an accident, *Brothers* certainly was. Students at a local
radio broadcasting school, given radio time as part of their edu-
cational program, interviewed me. But my statement about
Vietnam veterans was never aired. Instead, Stan Goff, also a
student at the school, heard the interview, and, without a word

to the other students, came to ask me to help him tell his story which, like those of other veterans, he felt had been suppressed.

At the time, as a professor at the University of California, I had organized the Vietnam Veteran's Oral History Project. Through the cooperation of Dr. Louis Starr of Columbia University's Oral History Research Office, I was able to have transcripts of in-depth taped interviews with veterans. It was a simple matter, through the labor of Elizabeth Earley of the Oral History Research Office, to add Stan Goff to the archives at Columbia. His account of his Vietnam experience was unique. With a Distinguished Service Cross, his photo blazoned across the *Pacific Stars and Stripes* for all GIs to see, he was an official hero in the seemingly "heroless" war in Vietnam. Yet his experience came out of a more universal experience in which thousands of black infantrymen played a formidable role. I felt their story should not be lost for they are heroes also. When Bob Sanders began to materialize out of the words of Stan's taped account, at my suggestion, Stan accepted his friend as a full partner in our joint effort. *Brothers* then began to emerge as an oral history of both the universality of the Vietnam combat experience as well as a more unique documentation of the ambiguities of heroic action and its consequences.

Clark C. Smith
Winter Soldier Archive
Berkeley, California

INTRODUCTION

Stan came to California in 1966. He had grown up in Tyler, Texas. He got out of high school at nineteen, and, as he says, "the draft was really on me." He had been raised by his grandmother but his mother lived in San Francisco. He figured that maybe since he was his mother's only son, if he went to San Francisco he might get some type of deferment on her account.

When I got to San Francisco, I entered City College. But things didn't go too well for me. My head wasn't really into the academic training the way it should have been. The basic truth is that in high school I didn't develop the type of tools that I needed to really compete in college. So I wasn't really a good student. I had a confidence problem. So automatically I said, "Oh well, I wasn't a good student in high school, so I'm not going to do too well at City College." I was convinced of that even before I got there. When the general education courses went too fast for me, I dropped them. I did excellent in music; I'd been an excellent musician in high school. But for the other studies, my confidence wasn't there. So I was subject to the draft. If you had a B average, or your father was wealthy, or maybe you knew a congressman, then maybe you could get out of it. I knew there were bureaucratic loopholes, but I couldn't get in on any of them. So I got my draft greetings. I just succumbed. What could I do?

Bob Sanders could not do anything either. In January of 1968 —at the time of the Tet Offensive, which was a turning point in the war in Vietnam—Bob appeared at the induction center in Oakland, California, scene of several angry anti-draft confrontations. Bob had been living in San Francisco, working for American Airlines.

When I got to the induction station, hell, I didn't know what I was doing. I just got there, and went through all the regular procedures, and got sworn in. I was sort of lost. At the time I was just about ready to get married to this black gal. She was pregnant and I was only twenty-one years old. I had been reading the newspaper, so I knew the war was going full scale. I would read about the draft and how many young Americans was going to Vietnam. It seemed to me about 60 or 70 percent of all the draftees were on their way to Vietnam. When I got my greetings, I figured I was on my way.

At the San Francisco airport I did unloading of the aircraft. I used to see all the gray boxes coming back from overseas with human remains. United, American, TWA were shipping them to all points. I used to load them myself. And I'd be saying to myself, 'Damn, man, maybe this might be me one day, coming through here, and my partners may be loading me here, shipping me home." It was kind of frightening. On my lunch break, I would go up in the terminal. I would talk to soldiers coming home from Vietnam. The stories I heard from them were scary. I learned later that most of the cats was telling me the truth. So when I got drafted, hell, I knew just about what was happening in Vietnam. When I got those draft papers, it really shook me up.

Stan

1 INDUCTION: FT. LEWIS

Arriving at the induction center in Oakland was very, very depressing. I took the bus over from San Francisco. There was the huge grayish building with glass all the way around that I'd been avoiding for months and months. You couldn't see inside. It looked bleak, and I cursed. It looked bleak because I was bleak. A few guys were standing around outside, but inside there was this huge sea of guys. They were sitting on benches like church pews, just like a congregation for young men only. It felt strange; here I was getting ready to be carted off. I was a black and I thought about slavery. You know, the guys were predominantly black. It's right there. You don't have to be academically accomplished to ask, "Aren't there any other races to be drafted aside from blacks?" At least 70 percent of the guys in my group were black, and I'm being very conservative.

In the room there was a general hum and murmur of people being processed. There was a big desk about twenty-five feet square. Names were called, forms filled out. It's called processing. I did a lot of processing in the armed forces. I did nothing but process all the damn time.

I saw Bob the first time inside of the induction center waiting to be processed. When I went to the front desk, he was sitting there staring at me. I was staring around at the mass of faces, and all of a sudden, our eyes locked. His eyes were very cold and depressed. I could almost see the hurt and anguish he was going through just sitting there. Maybe that was what caught my eye. I had no responsibilities myself. I wasn't married. I didn't want to be there, but what the heck. I had just come out to the Gold City of San Francisco and I wasn't having that many breaks. My mother was here but living in poverty. I saw that he had a "Why me?" feeling, and I guess I felt the same way.

Bob was sturdy, well-built, a very alert black; intelligence just written on his face. He seemed like a guy who would be very fluent with the ladies. I used to love to play around myself. When you run with another guy that you know has no problems about women, you can have a hell of a lot of fun. He sort of reminded me of myself. He probably thought the same thing.

When I saw him again five or six hours later getting ready to go out of the building, we looked at each other; no smile or anything. He was shaking his head and we both said at the same time, "What the shit are we doing here, man?" We'd been inducted; we were in the armed forces. It felt so cold and lifeless. It was like we were programmed to die, just going out there to die, that's all.

Anyway, we left the building and went on over to the USO. We were both a little reserved because I guess he didn't want me to think that he was harping on me, and I didn't want him to think that I was harping on him. Even though I liked him, I didn't want it to be obvious. It's sort of strange what men go through. I guess we were both wary of a leech-type of guy. I wanted to check him out from a distance. We were talking small talk across the room. We met another brother whose name was Jamie and were kidding him about his real nice Afro that he had: "He's gonna have to get rid of that Afro, no doubt about it," "Yeah!," "No kidding," "Right on."

Our orders were all the same. We were all going to Fort

Lewis, Washington. I'd never been anywhere but Texas and San Francisco; here I was going to Fort Lewis, Washington. Where the hell was that? Was that the state of Washington, or was that Washington, DC? I didn't know. Somebody said Tacoma. Shit, where was that?

We flew right to this Air Force base near Tacoma and were bused out to Fort Lewis where we were met by a little turd of a corporal, a little skinny guy with a crooked nose.

He waited till we got off the bus, and then he started hollering, "OK, God damn it, get out, you're in the Army now, stop slopping around, get your God damn ass over here." He was real young; had a couple of stripes on him. He herded us around in front of the barracks; told us "OK, God damn it, you gonna get all this long hair cut. You're in the Army now and all the bullshit stops." It was sort of a psychological induction. Getting ready to go gung ho.

A bunch of guys were milling around inside the barracks. Smoke was happening all over, and guys were finding out where other guys were from. Bob and Jamie and I were looking around at the white guys and we're talking about them: "Oh, man, look at these God damn guys; I wonder where they're from?" The whole group was about 65 percent black, and we're wondering how this was going to work out. Bob and I hadn't been around a lot of white guys. Jamie had been, to a certain degree. He was jumping right into it with those guys. We started hearing guys from the South, you know, from Alabama and Georgia.

Then all of a sudden, a pretty lively card game got started on one of the bunks. It was high card, not poker. I was watching the game with intense interest. I guess Bob thought I could play. "You want to get in?"

I said, "Aw man, I haven't any money." I was playing it off, you know. I didn't want to tell the guy I didn't know anything about cards. "Oh shit, man, here." I said, "All right, OK." So he handed me three bucks. I said, "I'll give it back to you, man." He said, "Don't even worry about it."

I got into the game and every time I bet I'd invariably end up

with the highest card. I just had some kind of luck. I ended up
with $140 right off the bat. And Jamie was doing a hundred
miles an hour. He must have won at least three hundred dollars.
Later he almost broke me up. When Jamie got through with my
butt, I ended up with about ninety dollars. Then the drill sergeant came up and yanked us all back outside and told us to
stand at attention. We were going to be issued our fatigues. We
thought we would find out where we were going to be stationed
at the fort. Actually, all we found out was that we were going to
spend the night in these holding barracks.

The next morning the drill sergeant started his routine, "All
right, shitheads, get out of those God damn bunks, right now,
on the double, move it." Oh, shit, we thought, it's getting started now. But we were pretty serious and alert, because we knew
this was the real thing. We didn't want to screw up right off
the bat.

We were really straight, square guys. But we did a lot of
growing up in the armed forces. We were really pretty innocent
about everything—government, society. We didn't want to
make any trouble. We went out there and did what this guy said
to do and tried to make the best of it.

Bob and I ended up in the same platoon with a black platoon
sergeant. We felt indifferent to this, but at least he was black.
We knew and know now that all the drill sergeants were bastards. They were the roughest men we'd ever met throughout
our entire stay in the army. They were nasty. I mean really
nasty. But it was due to that intense training that we even got
through the Nam. Seriously!

There were about forty guys in our platoon, about fifteen
blacks, fifteen whites, and ten other minorities. Drill Sergeant
Payne ran the 3d platoon—a Nam drill sergeant. I looked him
over. He was a flamboyant type with a thick moustache, tan
skin, lanky. Even though he was hollering and saying the same
bullshit as the other sergeants, I got a different feeling about
him; maybe because he was black. I don't know. Maybe this
guy was okay—maybe he was just following the rules and
wasn't a bad guy.

Drill Sergeant Payne was with us for a while, and then all of a sudden he was gone, disappeared, or transferred, and we had no drill sergeant. That was beautiful. Drill Sergeant Tadlock used to come over and put his foot in our ass. Then he'd go back and put his foot in his own platoon's ass. The other drill instructors used to say we were motherless. Tadlock was a very slim, very solid, middle–aged guy. He was about forty years old and fit as a taut fiddle. I really admired the guy as a great specimen of a man. I mean on the inside too. He could convey his inner spirit to us. We found that he was damned serious and very concerned about the men. We could read it in him. Even though he was very, very mean, we could tell that he was sincere. He felt that it was his responsibility whether we made it through the Nam or not. He felt that if he didn't teach us right, we were going to go over there and get mutilated. That was his thing. It wasn't us personally. He didn't care whether our name was John or Dick.

We would go out on long runs, all day long with a full pack. We ran to the mess hall. We never did walk on that fort at all. The only time we got a chance to walk was on Sundays. At night I would be hurting so bad I couldn't even go to sleep. I felt I was maybe dying, my body was undergoing such a tremendous change.

Doing all those push–ups was really something. I would think that I couldn't do but five or ten push–ups. Fifty push–ups? Nobody could do fifty push–ups! And all of a sudden I was doing eighty–five; no problem.

In the beginning of basic I couldn't run a square block without falling out. At the end I was doing the mile in six minutes flat. Six minutes flat, me? That was unheard of. You know, not me, man. And I was doing it. That was what the drill sergeants made possible.

Bob and I were constantly feeding each other encouragement to perform and not drop out. There were times when Bob wanted to give up—just quit and go AWOL. His old lady was pregnant and since they weren't married, the army didn't give him an allotment. He was only making ninety–one dollars a

month and he worried about that. We knew that as draftees
we'd be going to the Nam. That was no secret, but I told Bob
that if we made it back, we'd be okay and running off would
only be trouble. He could get married when he went home on
leave so when the baby came the maternity thing would be
taken care of by the government. So I talked him out of going
AWOL. We really stuck tight. He was counting on going home
after AIT (Advanced Individual Training) and taking care of
everything.

Besides physical training, Tadlock would have us go out on
the range for bayonet practice. The guy showed us how one
wrong move and we'd be dead. We learned hand–to–hand combat, how to kill a man fast, how to break down a weapon and
put it back together. We learned how to fire the M–16 rifle and
the M–60 machine gun.

I remember one incident on the firing range. I didn't have the
weapon held right while I was firing. Drill Sergeant Meckler
came along and kicked me hard right in the side. He was a
racist bastard and I really felt like shooting him down. All I had
to do was just turn right around. That was what my mind
started telling me. And then I started realizing that I wasn't
playing any more. This was a serious thing that I was into. This
was reality. A man comes up who had the authority to just kick
me in the God damn ribs because he was who he was. All I had
to do was just roll over, and pull the trigger, and just blow this
motherfucker apart. I never felt that way toward anybody before then. But I just pretended like he was out there at that
target, and I blew him away that way, because I knew if I didn't
do it that way, all was lost with my life.

Out on the weapon training areas the atmosphere was different. The sergeants out on the range weren't hard like the drill
instructors. Most of them were into really teaching what they
were supposed to teach. We never heard any guy that had an
attitude out on the range. I guess he wouldn't stay out there too
long if he had.

The instructors were Vietnam combat veterans; they wore

their Combat Infantry Badges. We would listen to these guys because they had been over there. The instructors told us about the units they had been in, what type of recognition the unit received. They'd say, "I saw a lot of guys get it." They might say something like that to alert us to the fact that we had better pay attention. "You can go to Vietnam and come back, if you remain alert. The strong can survive." They were telling us that most of the guys that got it were the guys that slipped up some way, made a mistake or figured that they were Superman. We could understand guys getting it in an ambush. That was nobody's fault; who knew who was hidden inside the brush? But I'm talking about guys that got killed when they took things for granted. A guy gets blown away by not taking enough caution. So basically, they were telling us about their experiences in the Nam and what we should do to better our chances.

The indoctrination finally took hold. We got to feel that these people knew what they were doing. Vietnam was always talked about as a joke. Nobody wanted to be in the gloom. Once we were into the war mentality, and once we were on the base, psychologically our training got to us. Even though we didn't want to succumb to it, we couldn't help it. When you do something over and over again, you have been programmed. I didn't know it then, but the Army knew it. And I know it now. We were brainwashed. You tell me brainwashing don't work? Bullshit. It worked. No doubt about it.

We were ready to go to Vietnam. Nobody was crying about it. Nobody was depressed about it, except some pussy guy, you know, some mother's baby. At first, yeah, I was concerned. I was scared. Then I wasn't. For people to be able to do this to you, you know that some brains are around there some place. And the instructors were very smart, too. They might not have had the best grammar in the world, but these guys knew what they were doing. I found this out, and I started getting confidence in what these guys were telling me.

I remember going out to a firing range to train with an M-60, for instance. It was particularly interesting. The M-60 machine guns were set up in cages. We just did nothing but fire all day long. I remember being impressed at how devastating the weapon was. I had no idea that I would finally end up with it, but I was particularly interested to note how fast it fired. I learned how to break it down. In addition, I learned to fire the M–79 grenade launcher.

The grenade range also interested me. When we got there, we saw big concrete–cubed areas and walked single file down into this training zone to get ready to go into these concrete blocks to learn how to toss a grenade. Of course, we knew that everything was pretty serious at this particular range. Nobody was cursing at us. They were telling us, "Just single file right down here, take it easy," you know, almost polite. We felt very strange. Nobody wanted to frazzle us. Obviously, they didn't want to have us too hyper. The instructors had on special helmets that were painted red or green, and we thought, Jesus, what was all this? It was an open mouth type of an experience. We heard these fragments going off—BOOM BOOM—and someone would say, "What the hell was that?" And someone else would say, "What the hell do you think? That's a grenade, man."

Everything was very carefully planned. Only two or three guys went in at a time. Of course, before we went and involved ourselves in actual training, we would take a seat on these hard–ass bleachers, and receive a full indoctrination as to what we were getting into. Training with weapons always began with a classroom session. We would go in and learn the theory, then we would learn the practical applications. The instructors told us all about a grenade, exactly how many people it could wipe out, its killing radius, what a grenade was made out of — lead and steel and wire and obviously the powder in it. They told us that the only thing we had to do was pull the little pin out. Then hold down the handle. Once you turned the handle loose, and the pin came out, that was it, goodbye! I mean there's no surviving. Except if some guy throws himself on the grenade to save somebody else. That's the only way. What kills you is the fragments or maybe the concussion. If you're right on top of it, it will burst the ear drums, and that can kill you. But the fragments are what really do the damage.

The instructor told us of some guy that had dropped a grenade. He was killed and the instructor was half-mutilated. So he was telling us that we had to be *awfully* careful and not bullshit. If we did drop the grenade, we couldn't blame an instructor for pushing our ass in there on it trying to get his ass out. He told us, "It's you against him, if you drop that fucking thing."

When we actually got ready to go into the concrete cubical, the instructor only took one guy at a time. I was sort of paranoid about it. I wondered if I would drop the God damn thing. That was a very critical point in my training, as I remember. When I got to the Nam, I didn't think anything at all about the fact that the grenade was on my ass, because I felt protected with them. If I saw Charlie—pshewooo—hey, man, that was the quickest thing in the world, you know. They could wipe five or six guys out. And the thing about it, everybody was afraid of a grenade—*everybody*. Hell, he could be super. He could be green. Charlie, anybody. When you see a grenade coming at you, man, that's like it's over.

It was sort of schizo–frantic for me to be sitting there waiting, when I'd never handled one before. I'd heard all kinds of stories and seen grenades tossed in all kinds of World War II movies. Then I got to the cement cube, tossed my first egg, and it was all over. Actually, I wanted to toss some more. It was that simple. The instructor smiled at me, once he saw I was steady and there was no problem: "See, it's not that hard. It's very simple." I guess throwing the grenade was one of the scariest and most exciting moments in training.

Basic ended on a Friday, and on Sunday we were going to another part of the fort. My orders were written up for AIT (Advanced Individual Training) at Fort Lewis. Bob's orders were also. That was where we lost Jamie. He went down to Fort Benning, I think it was.

The next day the drill sergeants hauled us out of the barracks, and Tadlock gave us his farewell speech: "We've trained you all. We know that we've given you the best training there is. You're going to go perhaps to another company that is not going to be as sharp and strict with discipline as we are. We know that basically wherever you go, you will be able to handle any type of circumstance. You should be able to, anyway. God damn it, I know damn well that I've put it into you. If you don't succeed, then it's your own God damn fault. And remember, there's only two kinds of guys in the Nam—the quick and the dead." And with that, the bus came. "Awright, God damn it, here's that bus, get your God damn ass outa here." That was it.

Tadlock was a very proud man. I never will forget how he stood there when we left him. His hands was on his hips and he was just staring at all of us, head never did move. I could tell he was just looking at all of us, and I guess he was just deciphering —who was going to make it back, who wasn't. Then he turned around and walked away.

We were ready for anything. Even though they said AIT was going to be a lot less hassle, we thought, bullshit. We were lined up in formation. Some guy came out of the CO's office, some kind of a special NCO that went to an NCO training school. They were losing so many sergeants in the war, they had to start this special NCO school, like Officer Candidate School. These guys would come out of the NCO school like E-6s. So we had one that was going to be the company sergeant E-6; "acting first," they called him. I never will forget this son of a bitch. His name was Rocky. He was like an All-American, you know. The crewcut, blonde hair, blue-eyed kinda guy. They're hyper. He took over and started hollering. "All right, FALL OUT, N Company." We fell out, and he gave a big bullshit speech about AIT. Then the regular drill sergeants finally all came out and we went back to our companies.

We got a black drill sergeant, Drill Sergeant Williams. Bob loved Drill Sergeant Williams. He was a very relaxed type of guy. It didn't seem like anything fazed him. He was an E-7, a combat veteran, a real pro. I think he said that he had been to

Vietnam two times. He had earned his stripes the hard way—
not like some of these "special" little buck sergeants. They
couldn't tell him what to do, obviously. He had all this damn
seniority, and like I said, he was a "field first" anyway. As company first, he was over Rocky, the acting company first. The
rest of the drill sergeants were also black, which was very
interesting.

Advanced Individual Training was predominantly black.
That was why they had all those black drill sergeants, probably.
Nothing but black guys in the whole fucking company. That
was particularly alarming to Bob and me. In fact, word was
going around, and it wasn't a quiet word, that blacks were
being drafted for genocidal purposes. Just to get rid of us—to
eliminate the black male. And we believed it. There was a general consensus in 1968 that there must be a conspiracy against
black youth. We didn't see any black officers coming out of
training; we didn't see any black NCO trainees coming out. We
saw lots of black drill sergeants, and they were all infantry, and
they all had their Combat Infantry Badges. They had earned
their stripes the hard way in Vietnam.

I think that those black drill sergeants had compassion for us,
which is why they didn't just get right down on us, not super-
hard. I know a lot of times I felt proud for Williams. He was in
for discipline, there was no doubt about that, as all the black
drill sergeants were, but they didn't grind us in the dirt. I didn't
know it then, but I know it now. They understood the racial im-
balance; all these black young men that they knew were going
to end up on the front lines. They wanted to make sure that we
got our training. Bullshit they didn't put up with. No doubt
about that. The punishment that I did get was not from any of
the black drill sergeants. One day, I passed the CO and I didn't
salute him. I didn't see his fucking bar. And he had me stand
up there and salute a damn mirror about four hundred times
while he stood next to me: "Good morning, sir. Good morning,
sir, good morning, sir. Sir, good morning." I felt so God damn
embarrassed. That was the only time I got punished in AIT.

In AIT we didn't worry about the drill sergeant coming around at night. We could also walk on the post at night. We could walk to the doughnut stand and have coffee. We could go and down a beer after training was over. It was much more relaxed. As a matter of fact, I had a lot of fun in AIT. I mean, we could go inside of the recreation center to shoot pool and play cards and bullshit and watch TV. That was after training was over. And as we went into the training more and more, they got more relaxed with us. I could have got into the band, but the guy wanted me to re-up for one more year. I was very interested in music, but I wasn't about to sign anything at all. On the weekends we got a chance to go to the clubs. We even got a few weekend passes to Seattle. I remember we met a young lady going into a club in Tacoma. We tried to make a pass at her. She looked down at our service shoes and threw her nose up at us. I wouldn't forget that.

Pretty much of AIT was review but it was all practical application. The whole idea was to enable us to know how to take care of ourselves. We were learning to read maps and use the radio. We had to be able to orient ourselves and survive. In the last class they said, "You're going to play hide and seek today. The game involves all of the training that you've had in basic and some training that we've given you in AIT. We are going to put you out on this range, and you are to try to get across without getting caught. That's all there is to it."

They drove us in trucks all the way out to these very dense woods in the middle of nowhere. There were lots of trees so tall you couldn't even see the tops of them; woods so thick that it seemed like an endless forest. I'd never been in woods like that. All they told us was which way to go without even a compass. And they told us not to run in groups because we'd be more easily detectable. "Either go by yourself or stick with one buddy," they said. We had to get through the obstacles in a certain amount of time. They told us that there were special assault teams that were made up of guys that worked on the range. These kids had Vietnamese clothing on. Their job was to try and kidnap as many of us as they could possibly find. They had concentration camps set up on the range for the guys they caught. At first a lot of guys were taking it as a joke. Then some got caught, and we heard guys screaming. And we knew it wasn't no bullshit; it was serious.

I started out with three other guys just walking in the direction I thought I was supposed to be walking. I'll never forget those trees that were fallen down; I had to walk on them. I thought I heard somebody coming at me, and I was down off the tree and hidden at the bottom of it. I stayed there for I don't know how long — maybe thirty minutes or an hour. I looked up and saw some of my own guys. I waved my hand and whispered, "Where are you going, man?" "I dunno, man, which way do you think it is?" "I think it's in that direction." "Hey, man, they caught some of those dudes; they ain't bullshitting." "I know, I heard some of those guys yelling." "Let's go, man." I left the other three guys and, miraculously enough, I ended up getting through by myself.

They had a few degrading things available for the guys they caught — basically just semitorture. They didn't break anybody's arm. They might have put a bit of cow manure on some guy's face, or had him in a ditch of water, or hanging up in a tree. They might have had him in all kinds of uncomfortable positions, bullshit like that. They wanted everyone to know what it would be like to get cut off from your unit. What would we do? A lot of guys got lost in those woods. I remember they were all into the night looking for some of them. Apparently there were just enough square miles to get us lost, but also enough for them to find us. Anyway, that was the biggest event in AIT.

At that particular point in time, I started asking myself: "How do I feel about actually being ready to go? Can I protect myself when I go to Vietnam? Do I know enough? Do I have enough confidence in myself after AIT?" The answer was a resounding, yes. I felt that I was ready. I felt that I could protect myself. I knew what I was doing. Obviously, there was still a risk of getting wasted, but that was a chance that I would have to take. Hell, if I walked down the block I could be killed. Or, if I walked down to the club and got into it with another GI, I could be killed. I felt that I had all the tools that they equipped us with. If anybody stood a chance, I did. I was going to get back. I was psychologically ready to go. I'm not talking about the bureaucratic military government or me liking it. I'm talking about the confidence in what I had been taught. I'm talking about being prepared mentally for war; they had done it. I could only say, "Hell, they must know what they're doing." Undoubtedly I would not be of sound mind if I said they don't know what they're doing, and then said that I was ready to go over and die. I was ready to go over and survive.

I knew I was going to Vietnam immediately after AIT. Bob wasn't. I was drafted in January of 1968 so I knew I would go in March. I didn't have any consciousness of larger issues other than what I heard through the broadcast media. I knew there was a large offensive occurring in Vietnam. President Lyndon Johnson had drafted sixty thousand men. That was one of the largest drafts that he had had at one time.

I went on my thirty–day leave from Fort Lewis back to San Francisco. I had a sweetheart, so I primarily remained in her arms until the end of my leave.

My last night at home I packed my things. I decided I was going to carry my trumpet. I love music and played trumpet in high school. I don't know what compelled me to carry a trumpet, because I knew that I was going to be out in the boonies. It was just some small voice, like God or my inner soul, told me to carry it. I put the trumpet inside my duffel bag. Also, I carried my mother's priceless collection of albums. I could never understand it. Anyhow, I guess it must have been my immense love of music or my last touch of reality, of who Stan Goff *really* is.

At the Oakland Army Base I was checked in and assigned a bunk. I put my duffel bag on my bunk and I put my albums inside of this locker. But the locker wasn't locked. Then I went out to get something to eat. It took me about an hour to find out where the food was. After I ate, I came back to my bunk to change, shower, what have you, and the albums were all gone. I mean, I was really in a lot of distress. That really depressed shit out of me. I had some feeling that I was going to take my mother's albums to Vietnam and have some use for them there. They were a priceless collection with great singers, Jackie Wilson, Earl Garner, Sarah Vaughan, all sorts of great classics that she had collected from the forties. She didn't know that I had them and I knew she was going to kill me. Here I was, about to go to Vietnam and I was sitting there thinking about dying by my own mother's hands. It was sort of traumatic for me. I was really depressed. I thought, "If I get my hands on that fucker, I'll kill him." I searched in my bags quickly to see if my trumpet was still there, and it was. I got a lock, put it on my locker and tossed it inside. Then I found out that the next day I was not going to be allowed to leave the base. I was here with maybe four hundred guys and I didn't know any of them. But we were all shipping out together to Cam Ranh Bay. I had hoped Bob would be with me but I lost him when he went off to Jump School at Fort Benning—not that he wanted to. It had happened by accident, you might say.

In the middle of basic training, a representative from Airborne School appeared. He told us, "If you guys are interested in airborne training, we'll talk about it. Then we'll sign you up for it. Give me your names." Bob and some of the other guys went with him to the cafeteria. I just said, "Naw." He told them what a proud unit it was and all that shit and they should put their names down so at the end of basic, when he came back, he would know which guys were interested and if they still wanted to, they could sign up then.

That's the way Bob told me it was. He really only went in to the cafeteria to get out of drill. Believe it or not, the roll sheet he signed designated which guys were to go to Airborne School. So that's how Bob enrolled though he didn't know it at the time. Bob thought he was going home on leave after AIT like the rest of us. Towards the end of training he really started getting

happy. We had been in basic six weeks and then nine weeks in
AIT and Bob was desperate to get away from the army. He
wanted to go home and marry his girl. Then if he had to go to
Vietnam, we'd go together, maybe be in the same unit. When he
heard he was going to Fort Benning, he was really pissed. He
told the sergeant there must be a mistake. The sergeant said,
"Do you remember when you were in basic, you signed papers
to go to Jump School?"

"I didn't sign to go to Jump School. What I did, I signed for
the interview with the guy to talk about it."

"Well, I am sorry. Your orders are cut for Jump School at
Benning. Jump School is only three weeks actual training with
two or three days of introduction and two or three days after
for shipping out. It takes about a month."

Bob insisted it was a mistake and he wasn't going. But of
course they couldn't change his orders just like that. The only
way he could get them changed was to go to Columbus, Georgia, see the commanding officer and explain to him what had
happened. The officer would have new orders cut and then they
told Bob he would be sent home on leave and probably from
there, get sent on to Vietnam.

There was nothing else to do. I went home on leave. We said
our goodbyes and I told Bob I'd see him soon. He got on the
plane for Benning. It was lonely after being together all this
time.

Stan

2 IN-COUNTRY: THE BOONIES

When we got to Cam Ranh Bay, I walked out of the plane into the heat and that humid air. This place felt like an oven. Man, how was I going to survive in this? I got off the plane and saw this huge base. I looked at the terrain and saw the red dirt and those low rugged hills in the distance. But primarily I saw the base. I was processed into this base as if I were just joining the army.

The base at Cam Ranh consisted of a lot of tents, dozens of wood structures which were officers' headquarters, and a few mess halls. All these structures were made out of heavy wooden beams with sandbags on top of those beams. It had been raining so that the red dirt was all wet and muddied. The sergeant said, "Don't be shy of the water, you are in the infantry. Don't be trying to step around the water, might as well get used to it."

So I stepped right into the puddles of mud and water; couldn't get around them anyway. I was a grunt and started acting like one. Everything was all laid out in our orders. I was in Bravo Company, so I went to B barracks.

The next day when I fell out with my unit at the designated
time and place the captain announced, "You're going to Chu
Lai." In-country orientation was two steps removed from the
boonies. I was not in the actual jungle, but I was getting closer.

Every morning I went to "actuality classes" which consisted
of a rehearsal for the experiences that we were going to encounter
in the boonies. For example, there was a class on plastic explo-
sives. It looked like putty. You could put it on a door and blow
the door and half the wall away. That was an all-day class.

We were given further instructions on how to survive at night
by going out on a simulated night patrol. We were told how to
fire weapons at night, just to see how tracers worked. We were
given instructions on the terrain, what to look for, how to survive in case we got lost, the type of animals that were around,
how to handle snake bite, what to do with a mine, how to
handle a pungi stick in case we stepped on one.

All the instructors were combat veterans. These were short-
timers who had been out in the boonies, and were getting ready
to go home. They would give us war stories; that was what we
wanted to hear. They would tell us about how they got hurt or
about particular incidents—how Charlie overran their unit one
night, something like that. We found the guys were very
friendly. You know, nobody was really ready to kick our ass
because we didn't salute or something like that. That was
dropped completely. Obeying orders was just automatic—but
having a relaxed rapport with our superiors was where it was
all at then. That was what they were teaching us really to do.
Even when the general came, we didn't have to stand up. We
were going into the boonies and we were expendable. One
wrong move and we were dead. They told us, "We're trying to
get you guys to understand the buddy system, communicating
with each other. There can be no friction out there." If a guy
that hates you is in back of you with an M-16 and you get in a
fire fight, he can easily blow your head off.

I remember this one particular incident one night after class
was over. I was getting ready to crash. I was just about asleep,

when all of a sudden I heard a "boom," and then the siren went off. In the classes they told us the siren meant we were getting hit. I heard some guy say, "Mortar attack." When the sirens went off, we were supposed to run out of the barracks and into the bunkers. The bunker was a very low to the ground structure, about four feet high. It had sandbags all the way around and on top of it—stacked about three to four feet high out from the side. It was open on both ends.

I ran inside of this bunker and hunkered down. Maybe some of the more elaborate bunkers were made out of concrete for officers or for a general, but most were just made out of wooden beams and sandbags. It would protect us, unless we got a direct hit. Even a damn cement bunker was not going to survive a direct hit from a 155mm shell. Hell, no. But I didn't know it at the time. I thought we were really getting hit. I said, "Oh shit, God damn, are we getting attacked, man?" The guys in the bunker said, "No, man." I said, "Listen, man"—I started hearing "BOOM, BOOM, BOOM—" you know, all over the place, and I said, "Hey man, we getting hit right now, man?" "No, man, those are our weapons." Then I started distinguishing the sound of the rounds being shot from the base from the rounds that exploded on the base. We got hit with about three to five rounds, but I was told that nobody was hurt or injured. I thought about my family at home that night.

After the in-country training, I went out to the 196th Infantry Brigade. On that fire base, I saw howitzers, 155mm guns. I saw tanks all over the place, a lot of sand, a lot of bunkers. I saw a low structured building, the processing building. We were to leave all our things inside our foot locker in that building. That was where I had left my trumpet, clothes, extra fatigues, everything. I filled in all my personal papers, who my things were going to go to when I died, if I died. They issued me a rucksack and told me to pack what I was going to need for the boonies. At that particular time I was issued my weapon.

There was nothing else going on at the support base—no classes, no orientation. I was ready to get out into what I had been trained for. I wasn't gung ho, but I was ready to go. If it was inevitable, why prolong the agony of wondering when the hell I was going to get out there? That next morning we were going to be shipping out to Bravo Company of the 196th Light Infantry Brigade. Little did I know, I still wasn't going to my company. That's what I mean by all this waiting.

Where the hell was I going? Who was I going to be with? How was I going to get there? I wanted it settled in my mind. The lieutenant in charge of issuing equipment told me where my hootch was, and I just sat around with other greenhorns. We said to each other, "What's happening, man, how you doing?" We were getting ready to go out and fight a war, but nobody was really doing that much talking. The only excitement I heard was from guys that were short-timers, the guys that were getting ready to be shipped back home.

Later on that night, the rest of the group started coming in. They were scattered all around the base, probably in Chu Lai city itself, or the USO, or one of the other tents, gambling. I found that out just listening to their conversations. There in the boonies 9:30 P.M. was pretty late. No one wanted to be out unless he was in a hootch up in the city with some broad. That used to be frequently done too. But I didn't know all of that. It took a lot of balls; but after a guy had been in the boonies, it was nothing for him to be moving around in the dark up in Chu Lai city. Even though there could have been VC and NVA up there, he had his weapon. If push came to shove, damn what was gonna be punishable. He'd open up on anybody that screwed around with him. I mean, it was a matter of life or death then. It was nothing for those guys to do that. But at that particular point in time it was all strange to me.

Being called "green" was sorta like a put-down. I felt, heck, I *was* green, so what? I didn't take it personally. But I didn't feel anybody really rushing to put their hands around me and say, "Well, listen, man, this is what's going to happen to you." I guess it was the short-timer's way of letting off their own frustrations and showing their own anxiety in getting the hell out of there. At that time I felt that there were cliques. The guys that fought together and had been in the boonies together were all around each other, and I could understand it. So they were sort of looking at us like, "You have to go out there and prove yourself like we did. You got to go out there and see if you can survive, like we did." I felt respect for that, and I really tried not to take it personally. Anyway, that night in the hootch I was hearing conversation about all the adventures that had probably been taking place all that day. I can still hear it. "Hey, man. I was just in town. I had a fine little old broad up there, man. I just got back." "You gonna get your ass blown away up there, man." "Aw, shit, I had my weapon with me. I wasn't worrying about a damn thing. Charlie probably in the next room fucking himself." Or, "Hey, man, we had a pretty hot game. Old Al and Rick and I, Jerry, and shit, Bill was in the game, too, man. My last hand I won thirty dollars. I won about four hundred dollars." Those dudes were gambling hard, really picking up some money. Three or four hundred dollars was really a win. They were having fun.

Later on that night, about one or two o'clock in the morning, we heard shelling. I woke up and was sitting there watching the movements of the other guys, and one guy said, "Hey man, don't worry about it. Those are our guns." They were 155mm weapons. They were so loud, they sounded as though we could get hit. Evidently, they were pouring out fire support to our men out in the boonies or maybe harassment fire against Charlie. They were hitting some AO (Area of Operations), there was no doubt about that. They didn't just fire 155 mm weapons. I think each round costs almost a thousand dollars. It might have been in excess of that. Anyway, those guys, to a new guy, sounded as though we were being hit. They must have fired about fifty rounds. Afterward, I stayed sitting on the edge of the bed just thinking, instead of going back to sleep. Before the shelling I had written a letter back home. I was lonely. I told my grandmother that I was in Chu Lai and I was getting ready to go out in the boonies. I thought the next day I was going to be out there.

That night, I never will forget. I had a dream about being out

in the boonies already, and the NVA were shelling us. I was
running around with my M–16 in my hand; I was really fighting in the war. I was running, diving back behind barges and
dikes and shooting as though I was really out there in the thick
of it. Charlie was running all over every place. Of course, a
common word then was "gook." The gooks were running in,
trying to stab me, and I was fighting them off with my hands. I
woke up in a cold sweat. I guess I went back to sleep quickly,
because then it was the next morning and the platoon sergeants
were calling us out. I didn't feel like I had slept at all.

All the green GIs were over to one side, and all the short–
timers, or the guys who were hurt, were in formation on the
other side. They told us what time we were going to ship out.

After chow, the green guys assembled on the other side of a
small landing strip. There was about fifteen of us there. Here
again, the waiting, the waiting, the waiting. . . . All of a sudden
we heard this big clamor of blades going "bwm, bwm." It was
a Chinook, a huge transport helicopter, with giant double
blades. There's nothing like it. You can't say it looks like a plane
because it doesn't. It's a box–shaped design all its own, like an
overgrown shoe box. It has two blades and a support on each
end, like a flag pole with the blades on that. Then on the side
are two sliding doors. I'd seen pictures of them in training, and
I'd seen them flying overhead at my training center, but I'd
never been in one. There it was in front of me, about fifty yards
away.

An NCO on the helicopter yelled to us to come in but keep
down. The pilot got off the helicopter and pointed at us: "Come
on. Keep your heads down." Everybody was sort of wary about
the blades. We'd heard horror tales about that. We all had our
heads way down, almost hunched on the ground, not realizing
that all we had to do was keep low, but not that low. Inside, we
saw metal floors, canvas strap benches, with aluminum rails
on the sides. The fifteen of us sat on these seats. Then they threw
in a lot of mail and some other food supplies. Flying off and up
gave me a strange feeling. I felt as though I was in a huge eleva-

tor; all of a sudden I felt sort of sucked up as this thing was flying upward. They told us all to hold on because the doors didn't shut. Of course, the pilots were strapped, but we weren't. Up and away, we just held on.

I thought I was enroute to the field. I didn't talk to the other guys. I guess that was what they thought, too. But we didn't go to the field. That was when we began finding out—the closer we got to the war, the more on our own we were.

The buddy system has to happen. You start realizing that you can't get through not communicating. Guys started opening up. Blacks realize, "I'm stuck out here in the boonies, and the white guy from the South is stuck out here, and it's life and death, we'd better begin to erase all this coloration immediately." At first, guys are strangers: they're from different backgrounds. Their parents taught them that a nigger ain't shit, a nigger can't do shit. You can see it in their eyes. They look at you as though you're supposed to ask them, "What can I do for you?" You know? It's as if they're saying, "This is what I want you to do, boy." You just see it in their eyes and their actions. They sit back and have an offhanded look at you: "I'm going to be better than you, and I can think, and I'm smarter than you." Being from the South, I'd seen that look all my life.

On this trip, there were about five white guys, about six or seven black guys, and another two or three Puerto Ricans. The whites were from the South. I'd heard them talk to each other. I want you to understand that they were not talking to us. They didn't say, "Hey, man." They weren't friendly, and I wasn't friendly to them. The Puerto Ricans were mainly talking to each other. After about twenty minutes we landed at what I thought was going to be the base, and we were hustled off the helicopter by an officer: "Get Off. Right Now. Move It . . . Get Your God Damn Ass Out . . . ."

We had landed at a huge fire support base called LZ Ross. LZ Ross consisted of a lot of sandbagged bunkers, only it was much shabbier than the fire support base at Chu Lai. I saw big trucks on this winding dirt road on the landing base and huge cranes

busily at work. It seemed like they were clearing more area for
installing bunkers and hootches. A lot of activity: GIs into different work; building bunkers, filling sandbags. The guys looked
haggard. I learned later that some of those guys had just come
in from patrols. I saw three or four officers walking around in
their fatigues. The first thing everybody started telling us was
not to salute an officer. Charlie wanted to kill all the officers
and he could be anywhere and see us salute. So I could actually
walk by an officer and didn't have to salute. I also saw all these
Vietnamese people working at the base. Old papa–sans walking
around in white pajamas were working there. Old women.
Young women. They had these black pajamas on. I couldn't
really see what their bodies were like. They didn't look that
appetizing to me.

I was following the NCO to where Bravo Company was stationed. My company was out in the boonies. The only guys that
were at the rear in my company were the NCO and some guys
that were on R & R, or because they were hit, or maybe just gold
bricking. Sometimes guys had some kind of sham going. Maybe
they knew the NCO. There were all kinds of slick guys. A guy
would get out of the boonies anyway he could, and who blamed
him? That was a day he wasn't going to get killed. Anyway,
guys were back there for some particular reason, and if they
could, they were going to stay back there indefinitely until their
time was up. Then there were perhaps two companies protecting the perimeter of this fire support base. The infantry
protected the perimeter, so that's why we saw guys filling sandbags. Maybe a company was going to be there for two or three
weeks. They were actually working to protect their own ass.
The NCO obviously wanted us to do it, but, hell, if we did a
shabby job building that bunker, it was our ass.

I learned from the NCO that LZ Ross was just a stopover. I
said, "Am I going out to my unit today?" He said, "Yeah, you
going out to your unit. Don't be so anxious." I never will forget
that. That's part of my nature: I'm always anxious to get involved, to get going. When he said, "Don't be so anxious," I

went into an explanation thing as I always do. "It's not that I'm anxious; I just want to know where I'm going, what I'm going to do." "Oh," he said, "don't worry about it; you're going out there tonight or this afternoon."

I remember sitting there, with five other guys, waiting to go out into the boonies to my company. All of us were black. When the helicopter came, the supply sergeant came out of his shack and said, "OK, guys, here's your taxi. That's the one you're going to be on." We got on the helicopter, and one of the door gunners said, "OK, now, I want everybody to relax. Remember, when you get to your AO, just keep your head low and run like hell. OK, just run. If you get under fire, just hit the dirt. Understand?"

There were two door gunners, one on each side of the helicopter. The gunners each had an M–60 pig. That was in some of the really early Hueys. Even though it was very hazardous duty, these guys volunteered as door gunners because there were a lot of sweet things that they could get. They were treated differently. They didn't have to worry about any CO embarrassing them for anything. They had beautiful bunks and hootches back in Chu Lai for when they got off duty. They might have worked all day. They might have worked eight to ten hours, but they were stationed in Chu Lai, and they got all Vietnamese women. Vietnamese women are very, very beautiful, as I found out later. They became more appealing to me the longer I stayed out there. Actually, any woman will start to look appealing. Anyway, those door gunners on those Hueys really had a sweet life, once they were off duty. They could get passes to go in to Chu Lai or Da Nang, especially if they had been in a hell of a fire fight, or got a big body count, or something like that. The black market was really a big thing over there; so they could steal all kinds of crap to sell to Vietnamese merchants for phenomenal prices, and make extra money. But a door gunner could get blown away at any time. If they survived, it was such a beautiful life. Guys were in line trying to be a door gunner.

That was the first time I'd seen a door gunner. The guy really looked gung ho. I mean, he looked proven. He might have had on a flak jacket and green fatigues. That was all most of the guys wore. No shirt, or T-shirt and flak jacket, that was all. He was going to put on more of an air when we got in there. He knew we were green. You listen to a guy like that when he tells you to stay low.

The highest casualty rate of new guys getting killed was when they landed into their first hot landing zone. The chopper would hover over the LZ. As they were dumping all the supplies out, the guys had to jump four or five feet. See, a lot of guys, they got freaked out. They got afraid to jump. After they got off the chopper they might stand up and get killed. In spite of the training, guys still panicked.

After we were in the air for about twenty-five minutes, we landed about three or four feet off the ground. We all jumped off, two of us out of one side, three out the other and ran like hell. I didn't hear anything at all. I was waiting for it. I just ran. I didn't see anybody. I didn't know where to run. I just ran straight forward. Then I hit the ground. All of a sudden, the men waiting for us appeared out of the woods. They stayed hidden purposely — if they were out there waiting around and they exposed themselves, Charlie could be ready to hit the helicopter when it came in. As I said before, we started finding out that we were on our God damn own. If we did get hit, there was nobody out there to say, "dive down, hit the ground." That gunner tried to help us, but he had to try to do two things. He had to try to put enough lead out there to save that helicopter, save his ass, and to help to get their ass. Also, he had to try to put enough lead out there so we could get on the ground.

On that particular day there was no lead, no nothing; we didn't get hit. Even though I didn't hear anything, I thought I'd just hit the ground for the hell of it. Then all of a sudden, the helicopter was gone. I stayed on the ground until I heard a guy say, "OK. Everything's OK. Ease up." So I slowly got up, and walked toward the sergeant, who was about ten yards away.

We were in a rice paddy. Always a rice paddy, which was about the only place where they could land. They couldn't land in the brush: they had to land some damn place. Sometimes in the boonies, when the helicopters came out, we had to chop out an LZ for them to land in.

My unit was near the rice paddy so I finally got to Bravo Company, 196th Light Infantry Brigade. But I didn't see the rest of the men. I thought, damn, where's the rest? I only saw the first sergeant, the radio man, and an E-6 that turned out to be the platoon sergeant. He was a fat first sergeant, and he was sitting there munching on some fruit. I found out he was a coward, too, but I didn't know that then. He offered me an apple. When I heard him talk I knew he was from the South. I knew I wasn't going to like him right off the bat. I just shook my head.

The sergeant told us to sit down. Why didn't we go ahead and take off? What were they doing? They were trying to see if we'd get hit before they started moving out. I didn't know that then. I didn't know what they were doing. After about thirty minutes, we walked over to another group of fifteen guys, mostly blacks, a few Puerto Ricans, and two or three white guys. It was the 2d platoon, which was going to be my platoon. The rest of the guys were inside of a nearby hootch. This was a Vietnamese hut. They were spread all over the hootch, sitting there like they owned the place, had their legs all crossed up on their chairs, just like around their living room. The mama-san and papa-san were outside cooking. GIs are something; just invading the property. Nobody said "come in," just went in and sat down. As we walked up, one of the sergeants said, "What are you doing in there; trying to get some pussy, I bet." Some of the guys started laughing. They answered, "You wanna fuck mama-san?" "Oh hell no, she's too old." "Not me, that's for the Sarge." This guy was an old E-6, sort of a weatherbeaten-faced guy. He was from the South too. So then the sergeant told us to pull out — "All right, let's go."

At that point everything I did depended on what they were

doing. So I just sort of watched them. They told me to walk real
slow, low down, watch for booby traps, and if we got hit, just
hit the dirt. We started walking single file. I was not assigned
a squad, but they told me to walk with 1st squad temporarily.
I walked with my weapon held at the ready position. We had to
walk many miles back to the company. I didn't do any talking.

It was strange to me to see the endless array of rice paddies.
We walked across these plantations that stretched as far as the
eye could see. The grass was green, beautiful, and thick. Then
we went across a bullet–ridden plantation with a once beautiful
mansion half blown to bits. We walked through a graveyard.
At first I was afraid to walk across a grave: it was part of my
heritage. You just didn't walk across anybody's grave as a
matter of respect, that's all. But there was no other place to
walk. The land was mostly flat with small, grassy knolls with
trees on them. The country was just beautiful; but I knew that
it was also deadly. I knew Charlie was out there. Anytime he
felt like it, he was going to hit us. I guess we must have walked
forty–five minutes or close to an hour. Finally we approached
our company. I saw the guys in the distance, and I thought,
Jesus, what a lot of guys. Finally I got to my company and the
NCO told me to go to the 2d platoon.

I met my platoon sergeant. "Hi, how you doing." "You're
Goff?" "Yes, I'm Goff." "OK. I tell you what, Goff, I'm going
to assign you to Ellis's squad over there. See Ellis over there?"
"Yeah." "OK, you're to go over and see Ellis; tell him you're in
the 1st squad."

So, I was going over to where Ellis was. He said, "What's
your name, man?" and started introducing me to the rest of the
brothers. All the brothers were sort of looking at me. They
opened up first. "Hey, man, I'm Baby–san, what's your name?"
"I'm Goff, man, I'm Stanley." "Where you from?" "I'm from
San Francisco." "I'm from Baltimore." "All *right*. That's Piper
over there: Piper's from San Francisco, is that right?" "Yeah."
"Hey, you got a home boy over here, Piper." "Oh, yeah?"
"Where you from, man?" "I'm from San Francisco." "Where

you from, Ingleside or Fillmore or Hunter's Point?" That's where the ghetto is. I told him, "No, I'm from Ingleside." "All right!" A guy from the same city. I thought that was pretty good. I figured he could really hip me. But I found out I was going to be hipped anyway.

The guys were friendly, "What's happening, man, how's it going?" Black guys. Almost all black guys. I met Baby-san and Piper, Castile, and Ellis. Ellis was my first guy that I really had any faith in. He knew what he was doing. He was a Mexican, real smart. Castile was a Mexican, too. They called him Hardcore. I found out later why. He'd wipe out a rabbit. Just a real cold-blooded dude. Steely eyes, he could shoot a twig off a branch a hundred meters away; he could hit anything. He was our point man, a mean guy. That was why they called him Hardcore. I didn't want to deal with him. With a guy like that, you'd have to go for broke. Nobody had an argument with him. I guess later on he found out that I was no easy nut to crack either, so we hit it off after that. He was always friendly, but I could tell he was sort of "crazy friendly." You've seen guys like that. They're friendly but you know they'll just go for broke on you in a minute. What I mean is that once they get off on you, they'll just try to tear you apart; so you have to have the same kind of attitude in order to contend with them.

I didn't know that then; but just because I was black, they were going to protect me like a brother, like a real brother. I would be protected just like a baby. They didn't just amble over but their eyes were on me. They didn't plan on letting me get wiped out. It's beautiful how that is. Brothers are really not that close back here in this country. It was amazing how the blacks were organizing among themselves over there. They really went all out to protect me and tried to orient me toward Charlie and toward the white men and why I was there.

Piper was very good at that. He was probably the brightest of all the blacks that I met in Vietnam, and I met a lot. He took it on himself to politically orient us about how the government was using us blacks. I have to give Piper a lot of credit because he really tried to make us realize what we were doing there, according to his way of thinking, which was that at all costs we must not risk ourselves and try to become heroes in this type of war. What is ironic is that I did just the opposite. But, as I said, his thing was "Fuck it, get your ass on the ground; don't try to be a hero at all. Try it only when you have no other choice. Don't try to go out there and volunteer for any God damn missions or some bullshit and get your ass killed." That was his whole philosophy. I sort of agreed with it to a certain degree. Then I agreed with it wholeheartedly from a black point of view. But I didn't believe in sitting around waiting till the shit hit the fan and there was no other alternative but to start fighting. My whole concept was that then it might be too late, man. But that was his thing.

At that particular time, most of the whites depended on the brothers to fight. That's how it got to be. And he and every brother knew that, too. His thing was, "Don't let them use you all the way into the grave." And that was what they were really doing. He told us, "The government is sending us over here. When we get here, we're doing the most fighting." Piper was trying to make us see how they were using us. Here we were doing all the fighting out of proportion to our number. Anyway, that's what he was preaching. That was his lesson. He was enabling us to understand the system as he saw it and to realize that all the money that was being poured over in the Nam could have been used to clean up the ghetto. He was politically oriented and just a hell of a guy.

I wasn't politically oriented. A lot of blacks were probably just like me — wondering what this government was doing. Why would they do it to us? Why should they constantly harass us and make us do stuff like that? We couldn't figure it out. But Piper said that what we were doing in the Nam made us like assassins. We were also their suicidal men. He made us realize that they could always get other blacks. That was what sort of hurt us. Piper had been in the bush about four or five months when I got there. He finally talked his way out. At the end of my term, he was going to go out himself, but he was still in the boonies when I left.

As I was standing there getting acquainted, the guys told me to take my rucksack off and start helping them. They were digging foxholes. They said, "Get to work, man. Come on over here, man. Shit, we need your help"—and then we got hit. All of a sudden, it was AK–47s, "didididididi, owee owee, dididi"—an AK–47 makes a chilling-type of sound. We all hit the dirt. It only lasted about twenty seconds, and then everybody was firing like hell. I wasn't doing anything, just laying in the dirt. Finally it was all over. It was a couple of snipers. We kept digging in. Everybody was complaining, "God damn it, why does that fucking CO have us digging out here in the wide God damn open?"

The CO probably felt that if we were going to get hit, most likely we could see them when they charged. If we were out in the open, they had to come out and get us. That was his whole rationale. Sometimes it worked and sometimes it didn't, because we got shelled like hell out in the open. It was just a matter of what the CO felt was more protective towards his men. You got support from the fire support base but it was hard for them to determine where you were when you were in the woodline. If you were in a wide open area, out in a rice paddy, they could decipher you from Charlie over in the woodline. But if you were in the woodline also, then it was hard for them to shell. They either shelled way over your head—no support at all—or shelled right on top of you. That was another good reason for being out in the open; but everybody was complaining because we could get picked off by snipers. Nobody got hit that day. That night the guys dug in as far as they could in case we got shelled. I just got in this deep hole and looked around. And Baby-san said, "Hey man, this is gonna be your home."

My first night in the boonies was pretty scary. Sergeant Ellis, my squad leader, told me we were going to go out on night

patrol. "I hate to take you out, Goff, but I need you. I don't
have enough men. You know why? We got hit last week, man,
and I lost two good guys."

I said, "Yeah." He said, "I might as well give it to you
straight; you don't want me bullshitting around with you."
I said, "Nope."

"I'll tell you what you do, man. You make sure that you stay
alert. Don't daydream ever, man. A lot of guys get out here and
they start thinking to themselves 'We haven't got hit for a long
time . . . ' and that's when Charlie hits you. Charlie lets you
walk around in a circle for weeks and weeks, and he waits until
your guard is down, then he hits you." He wasn't talking about
NVA; he was talking about Charlie; about packs of VC. "Hey, I
really hate to carry you first night out. I know you don't know
what the shit you're doing. But just watch me and stay low, and
by all means stay alert. OK? I'm begging you to stay alert."
I said, "OK. Don't worry man, I will."

It got dark. We got ready to go out, and I was nervous, man, I
was really scared. About nine o'clock, we went out. I said,
"God damn, anything can happen when I get out there." Walking behind these guys, I was flinching at every God damn movement. That was fine. The guys didn't say anything. That meant
I was alert, maybe too alert, and it didn't make them nervous
when every five minutes I was jerking around at some cricket or
something. We kept walking. The guys started bitching. "Hey,
man, that's too God damn far. That's far enough, man. Fuck it.
Don't go no God damn farther . . . I ain't goin' no God damn
farther." Then Ellis decided it was far enough. "Yeah, shit,
those motherfuckers don't give a shit about us."

Night movement, that was a suicidal patrol. That was one of
the worst patrols you could ever go out on. The purpose of it
was for you to walk up on Charlie and for him to hit you, and
then for our hardware to wipe them out. We were used as scape-
goats to find out where they were. That was all we were—bait.
They couldn't find Charlie any other way. They knew there
was a regiment out there. They weren't looking for just a hand-

ful of VC. Actually, they'd love for us to run into a regiment which would just wipe us out. Then they could plaster the regiment and they'd have a big body count. The general gets another damn medal. He gets promoted. "Oh, I only lost two hundred men, but I killed two thousand." In the states, people would hear that we lost twenty men when we actually lost two hundred. That was what happened. For a long time they were giving out body counts that were blown up out of proportion.

One time they put the whole God damn company on night movement. That meant that company was expendable. Orders that you had to go out came all the way from brigade headquarters. So, we went out, kept as quiet as we could. We didn't want to alert nobody. You found out it was your own ass out there. The smartest people didn't try to find anything. You didn't go anyplace. You just went as far as where you thought the CO wouldn't be able to hear you. And who the fuck in the squad was going to say any God damn thing? Because if you did say something, you could come up dead. I found that out later, too. Shit, even the sergeant might have known you weren't going out there. Even the CO might have known it. But as far as he was concerned, he was carrying out his orders. He was not going to say anything and you were not going to tell him. Nobody told me not to say anything, but I knew. It was obvious.

I never will forget one time when Piper was in charge of my squad on a night patrol. He was cussing, "God damn it, those motherfuckers, man—we gotta go on a God damn patrol, man." There was mostly black guys in the patrol; I think one white. I was still in 1st squad then; Baby-san was there, too. Piper and Baby-san used to protect me. Piper'd talked the CO into carrying a radio man. See, Piper was that smart. He said, "God damn it, I'm not going out there if we don't have a radio." So the CO made the radio man go. Even though he would have to turn the radio off because it made noise, we would have it in case we got into trouble. So Piper came back from the CO saying, "We got a radio. The motherfuckers didn't

want to give me a radio, but we got a radio. OK." Then we got
ready to go. Everybody was pretty gloomy. Nobody wanted to
go out there. You were just five dead guys if you found Charlie.
Everybody knew it.

About nine o'clock we moved out. Piper was pissed off. He
wasn't talking to nobody. Just looking at him I could tell his
mind was moving a hundred miles an hour. We got out about
two hundred meters away from the company, and the guy in
front of me whispered, "Piper says we're not going any
further."

"We're about two hundred meters out, man. What's Piper
going to do?"

"Piper's going to start firing his weapon. Now when he starts
firing, you start firing like all hell's broken loose, you know
what I mean? Then what we gonna do is, move back, and we're
gonna run like hell back to the company, you understand?"
"OK, fine." So we all followed his orders. At two hundred
meters out, all of a sudden, Piper started firing his weapon,
and popping grenades, "BOOM BOOM." Baby-san was the
grenadier. I started firing my M-16. "Let's go, man, move it,
they're over there, they're over there!" So all of a sudden, we all
started running back to the company, still firing all the way,
running like hell. Even the radio man was onto it and firing
like hell.

When we got back to the company, man, everybody was
asking, "Hey, man, what happened, any of you guys get hit?"
"Yeah, man, we got hit. Yeah, man, we must have seen about
fifty guys out there." "Is that right, man?" "Yeah, man."
Piper ran off to the CO. All of a sudden, the NCO told us to get
out on the perimeter, and he alerted everybody in the company.
We all started fanning out on the perimeter. The CO called
Piper over, and we thought Piper was going to get his ass court–
martialed. I don't think that the CO quite bought his story, because he didn't actually call for any fire support. There was no
shells, nothing. Piper told him that he ran into about fifteen
VC. We ran after firing; then he looked back, and thought he

saw maybe fifty men. That was the lie. Piper came back and
said, "Hey, man, we gotta go back up in front of the company
though." The CO made our squad go out about seventy-five
yards in front of the company perimeter. But we didn't have to
go out on a maneuvering night patrol, man, and just stay out
there for about three hours moving around. So that was why
Piper did what he did.

It wasn't like we were supposed to go out and set up. We were
supposed to wander around. Piper said, "Fuck that shit," and
came up with that marvelous idea. It was really a great idea.
He pulled it off, but I think they questioned the hell out of him
later. I guess men used to do that at first and not even question
it.

You got these word-of-mouth stories that went around from
company to company about the easiest way to annihilate guys.
Probably one of the highest body counts of GIs getting killed
was on night patrol. The second highest ratio for GIs getting
killed was ambushes. And most of the time they, too, occurred
at night. Booby traps were the third most deadly. Running into
an NVA regiment—that was the most dreaded possibility. But
I was even ready for that. Once you'd been psyched into that
"kill or be killed" syndrome for so many months, then you become hard-core like Hardcore Castile.

In the beginning, I wasn't anywhere near hard-core. That
first night with Ellis's squad I was scared shitless. And I didn't
go to sleep at all. Even when I was sitting on guard duty for
my hour, I was thinking about home. Ellis told us how to set
up our perimeter with claymore mines. We had claymores up to
the ass. When you got set up right, if you didn't panic, you
could really take care of a charge of fifty to seventy-five men.
They were really deadly. We set them out around us and I felt
pretty safe, believe it or not, with all that firepower behind me.
We had all the wires going in to the guy that was on guard duty.
And the guy that was on guard duty, all he had to do was just
detonate these mines and fire the pig. I also had these little
binoculars that I could see with at night. And I kept peering

around. I didn't see anything at all. Sometimes I thought I'd see something, and my eyes would be as big as they could possibly get. But it was nothing. And that was primarily how the night went. Nothing happened.

Bob

3 FT. BENNING TO BAO LOC

I'd graduated from AIT and added something else to the uniform. I was proud of wearing the blue rope on my shoulder that said I was infantry—the artillery guys wore red. I'd earned it because I'd taken all this ass-kicking abuse. Even though I really didn't want any part of the war, I was sort of proud of my accomplishments. Stan was already on leave when I got to Fort Benning wearing my dress greens and saucer cap with the army emblem and the shoulder rope. I had a copy of my orders and I had to see someone in authority to get them changed.

They started separating guys into different companies. Most of the people were holdover guys hanging around the barracks or guys that were permanent party. The first thing I heard from the airborne sergeant was: "What in the hell you fucking bums doing here with these bus driver caps on?" And I said, "What do you mean, Sir?" He said, "Don't call me 'Sir', you fucking asshole. I work for a living. Get down and gimme fifty." I wondered, what was wrong with this guy, was he crazy or what? He said, "Drop, boy."

Every other word, I found out, was "boy" — but they said it
in a way like, "Boy, get down. You gonna do so many push–
ups, you gonna push Georgia into Alabama. Now drop! Drop
that God damn funny looking cap off your head and get down
behind it and knock out fifty push–ups." I thought, what for?
But I learned in basic that if they told you to jump, you didn't
ask them why, you asked them, "How high?" Anyway, I
knocked off the fifty push–ups. I was really fed up. I hadn't
done anything to deserve this. So I was trying to explain to the
idiot, "Hey, man, I'm not really into your thing. I'm aiming to
get out of it, and you've got me doing push–ups right off the
bat." After that introduction, he reminded me, "We're paratroopers down here. We don't like our people wearing taxi
driver caps or bus driver hats in this area. If you're found
wearing it, you'll do fifty push–ups. If you're found with it after
I've told you once or twice, you'll do a hundred. Now, another
thing about this area — if you take one step, you hop, if you take
two, you'd better be in a full trot." We went over to the check-
in barracks where they checked your orders to find out who
all made the flight, and who went crazy or AWOL on the way.

After processing in, I asked another sergeant to see the CO. I
was told to shut my big mouth, he was the one who was supposed to do the talking, and who did I think I was? When I did
finally get to the CO's office, I explained my situation to the
first sergeant. I never did see the CO. The first shirt told me he
was in charge there. So he said to me, "Yes, we understand your
problem, but we have a slight problem, too. You know, paperwork is inputted into Washington, and it's gotta come back, so
we can get you out of Airborne School. But it's going to take at
least four to five weeks in order to do this. In the meantime,
what we'll do is have you at the holding barracks, down on a
place called Animal Farm. Incidentally, we had a guy hang
himself with his shoe laces down there last week."

So I thought this guy was really trying to intimidate me. He
was lying through his teeth. So I said, "Oh, man, say listen, I
gotta go home; I gotta be home in a couple of days." He said,

"You don't gotta be nowhere. Until your orders is cut, you can't be anywhere but here. Now, the thing you will do is this! You will simply wait until your orders come, and you'll pull details in the meantime. You'll mop floors and peel potatoes; you'll scour some pots, and you'll bust some suds down there. You'll do everything we want until your orders come through, if the guys down there don't kill you first. We got some rough guys down there. We got guys down there that got in trouble in Vietnam. That's where we send all our troublemakers." I thought the guy was telling me a lie. I was pissed like a dog by now. Then he said "It will take from four to five weeks." I was thinking, OK, if Airborne School was three to four weeks, and this thing was four to five weeks, hell, I came out better by jumping. Damn! They had me in a Catch 22 situation.

When I talked to a few people, they told me the guy was genuine. He was telling the truth. I would have to stay there because there was a lot of red tape involved in leaving. Being processed in and processed out took a lot of paperwork. And I didn't want to go to no Animal Farm. You know, I didn't want to go where all these cats hung themselves, and the details were so bad. I had enough of details in basic. Then another idea struck me. I'd been sending my girlfriend every penny I got because she was pregnant; she needed medicine. I had only enough money in basic to get cigarettes and a few necessary things. I thought well, in airborne I got fifty-five dollars extra a month for jumping. Right! By going through Airborne School, I'd come out better in a way, as long as I didn't kill myself! So I told the barracks sergeant, "Okay, I'll stick with the orders."

The next day they gave us orientation. They told us how proud we'd be in the Airborne; it was the best in the world. But they made us feel shitty when they said, "Now, which one of you scared–ass assholes don't want to go?" "You fucking yellow dogs!" I looked around. No one was holding up his hand. Nobody else was doing it; I didn't want to be obvious. Then they said, "The first one that does it, he's going to the ground with dirt in his face. I'm going to put my foot down his throat.

He ain't nothing but a yellow coward." So I thought, "Oh, wow, man, this guy's trippy. Well, maybe I've still got a chance to get out of this thing. Maybe after a couple of days of going through the training, I can fall out before they actually jump." But slowly I was getting to the point where it got to be a challenge. The training sergeant was saying, "I know half of you bums ain't gonna make it anyway, because we have really rigorous training down here. We're tough. I'll have you so that when I come in that barracks door at four o'clock in the morning, you'll be jumping out of your bunk saying 1000, 2000, 3000, 4000, looking for that rip cord. I'm going to push you to death. I'm going to push you till you puke. You ain't nothing but a bunch of maggots anyway. You couldn't make my class." I didn't like for people to dare me. So even though he wasn't really pushing me to the point where he was daring me, I just said to myself, "What the hell, I'm going through with it. I could use the extra money for the little lady. And for myself." So I went on through with it.

Man, I thought basic and AIT was tough, but this was the worst thing that ever happened as far as training was concerned; there was nothing like it. They moved you so fast through the training, you didn't know what to expect next. There was constant mental and physical harassment.

The first day, orientation ended at about twelve at night. Then they paired us off into the barracks. I was attached to 44th Company. At the very end of the orientation, this one sergeant got up in front, and he bragged that he was the best in the world; he was so sweet with jumping that he had something like five thousand jumps—he jumped in the day, he jumped at night, he jumped in the ocean. When he jumped he could land on a dime. He called himself a master blaster. He said he had more hookups than we got push-ups, and that if we listened to him, we'd be the best in the world. I recall the last thing he said: "Whatever you do, don't play with me, because I don't play. I'll teach you how to jump, but if you fool around . . . ." In a way, he was a good person. I could tell he was trying to be a hard guy, but he was telling us, "This is a dangerous thing; if you mess up, then you could kill yourself; it's nothing to play with!"

I can remember the first day real good. At four o'clock in the morning the sergeant walked in the barracks. I couldn't sleep that night; I was worried about the next morning. I didn't know if they wanted me to jump that day or what. I was naive. The first thing I heard was, "I'm not going to call you fucking assholes no more." He hadn't said nothing prior to that morning. And he said it as if he'd been calling us for ten minutes. He went on: "I'm not going to wake up fucking bums. You think I'm out here for my health? Get the hell out of them bunks!" Everybody came piling out, dudes from the top falling all over the place. "OK, get ready for the four mile run." I thought this guy was kidding. Four miles and it was not even breakfast time yet. He followed us out of the barracks and we went running round the track, singing a little song. He shouted and we repeated:

> HERE WE GO! (repeat)
> ALL THE WAY! (repeat)
> RANGERS! (repeat)
> WE CAN RUN ALL DAY!
> HEY! HEY! LOOK AT ME!
> RANGER! HA!
> GUNS! KILL! GUTS! KILL!

Whenever we'd run, we'd sing. So we were running like dogs; some guys were falling out. Whenever a guy would fall out, the sergeant would stop the whole platoon, walk back, and kick sawdust and dirt in the guy's face. Then he'd say, "Come and get this bum, he's dead," and then continue to run. Seemed like he was enjoying the run; the guy was even turning around and running backwards. I mean he was gung ho to the bone. We had to run every day till we got in tiptop shape. I thought I was in shape when I left AIT, but I wasn't in no kind of condition

compared to the training that this Ranger sergeant had in mind.
Whenever we'd run, we'd sing, and when we passed troops that
weren't airborne we'd chant:

> ON YOUR LEFT (repeat)
> LEGS! DIRTY LEGS!
> PUKE! PUKE!
> CAN'T BE AIRBORNE LIKE ME!!

The first week in Airborne School was ground week. This
was when you were exercising and you were going out to what
are called "mark towers." You'd run out to the training area in
formation. That was where you'd be doing a lot of simulated
jumping out of this low twenty–five–foot tower. The training
sergeants were teaching you how to hook up and how to mark
to the door. Basically, you were learning how to go out of the
door of the airplane. It was like jumping off a house. You were
in a harness that strapped between your legs, and when you
jumped, it gave your balls the sensation of your life. It was
worse than jumping out of a plane. When you marked to the
door, just like you were inside a C–119 with your parachute all
hooked up, you shuffled to the door with one foot flat and one
toe up. The heel and toe are just the opposite as you're shuffling.
The plane was naturally kind of swaying, and, in order to keep
your balance, you were sorta swaying. So they taught you to
shuffle; then you learned to jump out of the twenty–five–foot
tower on a static line with a harness on. It was like jumping out
on a reel, and when you got to the bottom of the line, it jerked
and pulled you.

In the morning we'd do the mark tower; in the afternoon we'd
do Swing Land Training. From there we'd go on to the PLF or
Parachute Landing Fall. They'd drop us out of the little swing,
and we'd bust our butt or the back of our head, because we
didn't know when they released us. We couldn't land expecting
to do a PLF, but we tried to hit on four points. The training
sergeant was there to check us out. The less we learned, the
more PLFs we'd do.

Next you went into tower week. They elevated you to a fifty-foot tower and all of a sudden they dropped you. At this stage you had a real chute on. In the meantime, you were going through classes constantly; you were being well prepared. In the actual training, you had these sergeants standing around giving you the rundown on how to land; they explained what to do coming down and how you could break a leg or your neck if you didn't listen. If you didn't follow their instructions, you could really hurt yourself. I found out they were right. You had to do it in a certain set way. Once you hit the ground, you had so many seconds to fold the chute up, crisscrossing, rolling up. Then you had a few seconds to get off the drop zone. They taught you how to guide the chute when you were coming down. Some of the guys, when they jumped, landed on another guy's chute. The other guy was safe, but you were in trouble because your chute was going to collapse as if you just hit the ground. So they taught you to just try and run off the other guy's chute. Or if you got tangled up, they taught you how to "bicycle," you pedaled to get unwrapped.

I remember a couple of partners got pissed because this one guy tangled them, and they was up there in the sky pissed and flailing at each other. The sergeant was down on the ground, and he was yelling at the top of his voice, "Get the fuck out of there . . . ." Tower week was frustrating and dangerous.

The third week was actually jump week. That was the scary week. That was when the fun began. I didn't think I was really ready to jump. But what really convinced me to go ahead was the plane we was in—an old C-119. They called it the Flying Boxcar. The damn thing was so ragged and shabby, man, I thought it was going to crash. Hell, I was glad to jump out of it. Really, man, I think they entice you to jump with that plane. I will never forget that day. On the runway, the sergeant was saying, "Now, make sure your equipment is ready." Make sure of this; make sure of that. They had riggers that rigged the chutes and some of the guys was saying, "Hey, maybe these guys didn't rig the chutes right. One little flip and you're gone." We had a little saying: "If the chute don't open wide, you'll be a spot on the countryside." And that stuck in my mind, you know?

If your main chute didn't open, you had a reserve chute that was harnessed in front. The reserve chute protected you against a rigging mistake. If you jumped and someone had rigged the chute wrong, first you might get a cigarette roll. That was when the chute would be rolled up like a cigarette and it wouldn't open at all. Or you might get a bra; the brassiere–type chute was where the strings were mistied. They would cut right through the center of the chute and cause it to double fold so the canopy wouldn't support you. Then you'd have to use the reserve. The reserve was a regular chute, too, only it was right below the suspender harness on your stomach. You had the main chute — the T-10 — on your back attached to a static line. As you jumped out of the plane, the static line would catch and your chute would automatically open; if the main didn't open, then you pulled the reserve. If that didn't open, then you had another thing that you could do. You could always put your head between your legs and kiss your ass goodbye. That was the way the sergeant put it. So that was on my mind too just before I made my first jump.

We had a thirty minute wait on the runway before we took off . . . maybe a hundred or so guys. While waiting, your part-ners helped you check your equipment. There were last minute instructions from the training sergeants. Some cats played it really smooth; some guys, like me, were scared as shit. There were maybe ten planes loading. When 43rd Company went, then you knew you were next, and you began to get butterflies. You got on your plane and, as the plane started rolling down the runway, the jump sergeant yelled:

WHAT ARE YOU?

AIRBORNE!

LEGS?

AIRBORNE!

I was trying to get myself fired up, but it wasn't working. As the plane climbed to about thirteen hundred feet, it was so damn noisy I couldn't hear nothing. But they had taught us the jump command. I couldn't hear the sergeant, but he would give hand signals like: "Stand up; Hook up; Check equipment." After everyone checked their equipment, he would signal, "Sound off for equipment check." Starting from the back, the last man would turn and let his partner check him and he would check his partner. Then each guy in turn would check the next man in front of him, right on up to the front. We had thirteen people on each side of the plane, and we had something like benches that we would sit on until it was time to get up. After the sergeant gave the jump command, and we'd finished the "Sound off for equipment check," the response came from the back, "OK, OK, OK . . ." all the way up to the front. By that time, the green light would be on. We were over the drop zone with so many seconds to jump. Once the plane got to the drop zone, if someone froze in the door, then that would cause a delay. All the pilot knew was that we were over the drop zone; that was when he would press the green button. He couldn't see nobody back there where we were, so it was up to the jump master to get everybody out while the plane was over the jump zone. If somebody froze or delayed, then he could jump into the ocean or the trees.

After the equipment check, the jump master would give the command: "First man, stand in the door." Then the next man would move right in back of the first, and so on. Then he would say, "Go!" We would start jumping about two seconds apart. After he told the first man to go, the next man was right there. Everybody was supposed to be coming out of the plane in a fluid motion. If somebody froze . . . Well, that was why the jump master wore them jump boots. When you kicked a guy right in the butt, he was going right out of the plane. I'd seen that happen. One guy froze in the door because it was his first time. He was scared. The jump master just peeled his fingers off; it was funny in a way.

When that first guy was standing there with both hands on each side of the door, his whole face contorted from the blast of wind. While he was standing there waiting on the jump master to give the command to go, he'd think of bracing himself against that blast of air. He wanted to be as tight as possible when he jumped, his toes pointed toward the ground, his knees together, slightly bent, not too stiff, but enough to keep them together once the blast hit him. He didn't want the blast of air to blow his legs open and start him flailing in the wind. He'd jump out toward the engine, and the blast would take him back underneath the plane. If he was flailing, he might hit part of the plane. His chin had to be tucked into his chest and his elbows into his sides, with both hands on the reserve; one near the reserve rip cord, the other one on the back end of it. That position would keep him tucked in. Once the blast hit him, he'd start to tumble.

In the four seconds that it took for the main chute to open, it seemed like four days. You know what I mean? I was ready to pull that ripcord on the reserve quite a few times. It seemed like it was taking too long for the main to open, and when it finally snapped, I got a sudden jerking sensation. When it finally billowed open, I said, "Thank you, God . . . ."

The descent was not fast at all. It was just like a swaying motion, down slowly, slowly, slowly. The last fifty feet, when the chute didn't have that much air underneath the canopy, you started to speed up. Once you got about fifty to thirty feet from the ground, you just fell. It was like jumping off a house. This was where the parachute landing fall came in. You hit and broke the fall with a roll—just like the rocker on a rocking chair. You should have come right out of it. One thing I didn't know when I first jumped was that you could actually land by popping the risers on the harness. You just held these suspenders down until the last minute and then turned them loose; it would jerk you back up, and you could land on your feet. But they didn't allow that. They didn't want nobody hamming it up. After you hit the ground, there was this sergeant on the landing zone giving orders. He was out there kicking and cussing, getting everybody off the drop zone. You got a thousand other guys above you about to jump. They would run something like twenty or thirty planes just one after another. By the time you hit the ground, another plane load or two was coming over. You looked up and saw nothing but thousands of canopies everywhere. So you had to run off. And the worst part for me was running that mile and a half off the drop zone with the chute. It was pretty heavy. You had to fold it, and, as you were folding it, you had to run toward the truck they had parked on the edge of the drop zone.

Five jumps qualified me for my jump wings—we called them blood wings. As we ran off the drop zone, we got in formation and they had a little ceremony. People kind of milled around, and then we got back on the cattle trucks and went back into the base. We moved from the training barracks to the transit barracks. That was when we got to *walk* around the area, go to the NCO club. In the meantime, they were working on our orders, which lasted from three days to a week. After I finished jump training, I felt proud. When I saw an officer, I saluted with "All the way, Sir," and he said, "Airborne."

But I still didn't know what the hell was going on. So I finished at Benning, got my orders cut, got my money, leave time, manifest for tropical clothing, and found out that I had to report back to Fort Lewis. Then I was like a late freight out of Benning; caught a plane into SFO. I finally got home.

When I did get home, I was really elated. As I came out of Jump School, Stan was just going to Vietnam. I went by his Mom's house to get his address. He had gone a couple of days ago. So I just missed him. All his Mom knew was that he would be with the 196th Light Infantry Brigade in Vietnam. She didn't know nothing about Vietnam, whether he would be in the Delta, or the Central Highlands, or what part of Vietnam. I had my thirty-day leave. Time to forget about Vietnam and the army.

After leave I was a married man but just the same I reported up to Fort Lewis, Washington, on 28 June 1968 and processed

in. Three days later I was on my way to Vietnam. During the
three days I was issued jungle fatigues and jungle boots, and
lighter camouflage stuff; all black stripes so you wouldn't be
noticed when you'd be walking through the jungle. Ordinarily,
uniforms have yellow stripes to designate rank; obviously, you
could see them further away—they'd be silhouetted like a neon
sign. Any military personnel in Vietnam would have to wear
either dark black insignia whether it be stripes or sew-on jump
wings or any type of rank, even on the collar. The officers
would never wear metal—anything that would reflect the sun.

At the same time that I was getting a change of clothing I got
a little orientation on Vietnam, like what to expect, but half
of the guys there was really just fountain pen fighters. They
never had been over to Vietnam. It was obvious. If guys had
been overseas in combat, they would wear a unit overseas patch
on their right shoulder. I didn't know if it was required, but if a
guy in the infantry had been in a combat zone and done any
kind of fighting, he would wear the Combat Infantry Badge.
The army put a lot of emphasis on our knowing the rank—so I
knew that most of the guys there were just processing clerks.

I talked to a few of the clerks and some returnees, and got an
inkling of what was to come. The clerks told war stories that
they got from friends that had been to the war, or they made up
little stories themselves to try and frighten you or intimidate
you, just to give you a hard time in general while you were
processing out. Maybe it made their job easier. These guys were
permanent party; they had eight to four-thirty jobs. They
talked all kinds of bullshit. They might even have bought a
medal in the PX and put it on their uniform—as long as they
thought they wouldn't get caught. The Vietnam returnees gave
me the truth. These were dudes that had got off the plane and
was processing back into the World. They knew I was going.
I wasn't just some kind of spectator that was curious and might
put them down as freaks. So they was trying to hip me to what
I was about to face. These guys were boonie rats and damn near
all of them wore CIBs. A few of them were paratroopers. They

could tell I'd be going to a paratrooper unit, possibly their own
—the 173rd, eighty-deuce or the 101st. They knew I was infantry and I'd be in the thick of the boonies. I would talk to them
just like I would talk to a friend. A few guys would be reluctant
to talk, but mostly these guys told me, "Don't get over there and
start half-stepping; stay alert when you get to the Nam. It's
gonna get rough; it's gonna get funky; it's gonna get nasty. But
you can make it." They'd made it! They said, "Guys that start
fucking around out there in the bush is gonna get their head
ripped; they're gonna get blowed away. Charlie is very dangerous. I've seen him, man. He's a professional fighter, and when
you get out there, there is no room for amateurs. If you keep
your shit together out in that jungle, you'll live." I appreciated
them telling me the truth.

I still had a lot of questions. I was told at Fort Lewis, since
I was airborne, that I would not be with a regular unit. On my
way up to Washington, before I left for Nam, I remember
wondering if I was gonna see Stan over there. I wondered how
big Vietnam was. I thought what I'd do when I got leave was
try and find Stan and hook up with him over there. That didn't
work out because we were separated by a lot of jungle and
mountains. Plus another thing, I was airborne. Since I was a
paratrooper, naturally I had to go to a paratrooper unit. Stan's
unit was "straight legs," a leg unit and regular army. I knew
right then I wasn't going to be with him, so I started looking
around for another partner. Lloyd Hill, a white fellow from
Monterey, and I got tight. We had been through AIT together;
when Hill's partner and Stan split from us, we teamed up down
at Benning. We finished Airborne School and later on, he and
I were stationed in Vietnam in the same company.

They sent us over to Vietnam on a C-141. There were no
seats in the plane. We had only our duffel bags. It was pretty
uncomfortable, two hundred guys sitting on and off their duffel
bags for twenty hours. You kept moving from the floor to the
duffel bag; your ass got tired and you squatted on your knees
for a little while. The plane was like a regular cargo plane that

was hollowed out. We got fed a miniature TV dinner, but you could tell that it was a mixture between C-rations and something they cooked up. It was on a little six-by-six tray; wasn't that much food on it. I gobbled that little jive up in a hurry. We joked about the service—the waiters. They picked out a couple of us, "Hey, you, you and you; get over here." So we joked with these guys, "You don't make a bad stewardess, honey." We laughed it off, trying to get our minds off the flight. The length of the flight was taking its toll—the longer we'd fly, the scarier it got. We made two stops. We flew out of McCord Air Force Base and stopped first for refueling and mechanical checks in Anchorage, Alaska. We took off from there for Yakota, Japan. I'd never flown so far from home in my life. I couldn't see nothing but clouds and every now and then when it was clear I could see a patch of water. I was depressed as hell anyway, but I was getting restless. Finally we landed at Yakota for a couple of hours—last chance to buy souvenirs in the terminal there—and then we took off for Vietnam.

The guys were talking on the flight the whole time. We were thinking out loud, "Hey, man, I wonder what it's like." We didn't know what the hell was going to happen. A million times the same thought was running through my mind: was I going to make it back? I'd be all right as long as guys was awake and I'd be bullshitting and jiving. Then guys would fall asleep and I'd find myself looking out the window, my mind wandering, what was going to happen? Were we gonna start fighting when we first get there? The army treated the whole trip as hush-hush and rush-rush; they didn't tell us nothing. As we were going further and further, I was thinking to myself, "When the hell are we going to get there?" We were flying, steady flying, just flying, flying, flying.

Finally we got there: Cam Ranh Bay. Just as we were coming into the landing field, we heard a lot of big guns firing. I wondered, oh, my God, were we going to be fighting right now? I hadn't got no weapon! How the hell were we going to fight? This was sort of like a dream. I couldn't believe it. Vietnam!

The terminal at Cam Ranh Bay looked like a long, thin shed. There were a lot of air force planes there — F-104s — on the ramp. I could still hear this firing. I was trying to figure out where the hell it was coming from. I found out later it was nothing but what they called H and I fire (Harassment and Interdiction). They did it everyday. It was a procedure, firing into the mountains to make sure there was nobody out there trying to set up mortars.

It was about four o'clock in the afternoon when we landed. And the heat, man, you couldn't believe the heat. It took my breath away. Between the heat and being scared, I didn't know what to think; I was just gone. They took us to the 22d Replacement Company at Cam Ranh. Nobody seemed to notice the howitzers that were still firing, but I was really jumpy. The sergeant told us that we wouldn't be going out to our unit for several days, so finally they decided to take us over to the holding barracks.

We started to process the next day. There was no talking. The sergeant said, "For sure, we don't want no talking here. We're going to process you bums in and I want you to understand one thing — there's only two types of fighters over here in Vietnam: the quick and the dead. When you get to your respective units, you guys stay alert. Forget about home; leave home right here — in fact, you can send home back home. Don't think about no girl friends; don't think about no father; think about what you're doing. Just stay alert. If you guys stay alert, you'll be turning these goods back to me at the end of a year." Then he said, "Don't think I haven't seen it. I've seen people with their heads over here and their bodies over there, on account of they're not doing what they're told. They're not alert. They just get out in the bush with their head in their ass, and they're not paying attention to what's going on. It's not my fault that you're here. I'm sorry to see you fellows here. But while you're here, you'd better try to stay alive, because this place is no joke. That little man out there, he's professional. He will get your head. All it takes is one mistake and you're gone. Now you guys go through here as quick as possible. Take your bedding and stuff. We'll have a sergeant come around and put you on detail, filling sandbags for the bunkers, building bunkers, whatever, until we can get you out in the field to your company." And that was exactly the way it went down. For a few days we filled sandbags. Cam Ranh Bay was a really secure place, sort of like Saigon. There was no kind of activity from the Viet Cong or NVA. Maybe just a few mortar rounds here and there.

We stayed at Cam Ranh Bay three days. Each guy knew which unit he was going to, because during the processing in they had read out the individual orders. "OK, Bob Sanders, you'll be going to the 173d up at An Khe." He put everyone going to the 173d in the same barracks; if you was going to Stan's unit, the American, you'd be in that barracks. The 173d was a brigade, and, in fact, it was reactivated from the 503d, which was a unit they called "the Rocks." They jumped into Corregidor back in the Philippines in World War II. The unit was reactivated for Vietnam. Most of us were paratroopers. They had us broken down into different battalions; some of us was going to regular units. But the main body was airborne. Some of my friends were sent up to the 1st Battalion at LZ English, and some went to second bat at LZ Uplift. The 173d were working out of An Khe in the Central Highlands.

The Highlands was a little different from Cam Ranh Bay, which is about one hundred miles away. Of course, I didn't see a map. I didn't know where Cam Ranh Bay was situated in relation to anywhere else in Vietnam. All I knew was that I had come from the United States. On the flight over I lost all sense of direction. I used the sun a lot because the sun always rises in the East and sets in the West, but I was so far from home I wasn't even sure about that. One of my partners asked me one time, "What's that up there, the sun or the moon?" and I said back to him, "I don't know; I'm not from here."

They gave us a week of orientation, which consisted of jungle school. It aimed to familiarize us with the terrain, booby traps, operations procedures, the stuff we'd be up against. They issued us claymore mines, hand grenades and rucksacks with extra pants, undershorts—of course, no one in Vietnam, except maybe the officers, wore drawers because it was too hot and cranky. In fact, your home away from home was on your back. You never carried anything except stuff that you would basically need—food, ammo, and maybe writing material.

Water was essential. They would issue you four fat rats, which were rubber containers that would hold a gallon of water each. They were balloon–type canteens—the more water you put in, the more it would stretch. A lot of guys used to hump those, but the thing about fat rats was that they were easy to puncture. They'd be hooked on your rucksack and a thorn could hit 'em and cut 'em. Then you got the ass because you lost some water. I'd carry about four or five rats and maybe four or five regular canteens. Water would have to last like rations. We were advised not to drink the water in Vietnam because of contamination. It was dirty swamp water. If you ran out, then you had to use the purification tablets with the swamp water. But we tried to avoid that. Later, when we got into the mountains, we ran across streams, and then water wasn't no problem. Down in the valleys, you had to depend on the water you carried, and nobody gonna carry water for you. So the fat rats came in pretty handy. Then they gave us a nine–day supply of C–rations. By the time they finished handing out what you needed, you had about seventy–five to eighty pounds on your back, plus your weapon and your ammo. You didn't want to be out in the woods without ammo. As we were loading up, I wondered what we were going to do with all this stuff. But I found out that I could carry that and more, if I had to. In fact, we used to hump for days with at least that much, and I mean just hump, man.

Finally it was time to get down. I said to myself, "Well, this is it, man. The real thing is happening now." They sent me to Charlie Company, 3d Battalion of the 173d located down in Bao Loc. When we landed, I looked out there and saw these ragged troops; they were dirty. I mean, man, they just looked

like something I ain't never seen before. I was thinking those
guys are really hard. My fatigues were still new. I wondered
what these guys had been through. Little did I know that this
was my unit. I saw a few brothers, so I said, "Hey, what's
happening, blood?" They didn't say shit. I said, "Hey, what's
going on?" Just greeting them. They didn't say anything at first,
then they said, "Yeah, you cherry, welcome to the Nam, you
fucking bum . . . I'm short, buddy. I'll be leaving outa here in
a couple of days. You maggots coming in to take my place? Get
the fuck off the chopper, get over there and get some supplies."
I wondered who the fuck this guy thought he was talking to. I
heard another guy say, "Yeah, look at the cherry." I was
thinking that these guys didn't even feel sorry for us. I couldn't
believe it. And they were saying, "Yeah, tell you one thing, you
better keep your ass down, cause Charlie don't play. He dug our
ass." These guys had just come off an operation for standdown
and had a few guys wounded. The only reason they came off
the operation was because a lot of guys were getting ready to
leave. So the company had to pick up the new guys and take
them back out. Even the CO looked scroungy. That cat looked
wild, not even shaved. I saw a couple of guys with ears around
their neck for beads. I was thinking to myself, "Damn, what is
this? These guys are animals!" And they were saying, "Yeah,
welcome to the Nam, you pigs."

I finally saw a couple of guys that looked cool, so I started to
rap with them. I asked this guy from St. Louis named William
Patton how it was. "Everything I been told, is that true, man?"
He said, "Man, it's worse. It's funky out here, man. Like we was
out there for eighty–three days before we came in for standdown this time. We're going to rest for three days, then we're
going back out." So, man, I was scared, I was nervous, I was
looking around for what they had told me was the beautiful
city of Bao Loc, and there was nothing. The "city" turned out
to be a few Vietnamese villages with hootches and huts. It was
disheartening. Our compound was just outside the village. The
compound was the fucking shits, man. We landed in the com-

pound and all I saw was canvas tents inside this wire. It was a fire support base which protected Bao Loc village. Our main TOC (Tactical Operations Center) was out of LZ English at Bong Song up north. Bao Loc itself had some rundown French buildings and I could tell that it had been bombed and shelled before. But we weren't even near the city; we were over a mile away. So I was walking around the fire base at Bao Loc asking guys what was happening: "What did you guys go through?" Then I stopped asking; I'd better find out for myself.

I knew the company was getting ready to go back out; I knew there was going to be heavy shit in two or three days. It turned out to be only two days. All of a sudden, two days later, the CO said, "OK, Charlie Company, put the shit on. Let's get out of here. B Company just got hit — they got four dead and sixteen dudes wounded. Let's get out there and help them." I didn't know what to expect. The choppers came in and we headed out. We found B Company but we didn't make contact.

Matter of fact, we didn't make contact for the next three weeks, which was a blessing in disguise. It gave me a chance to get used to humping and get acquainted with the rucksack. Hill was in another platoon, so I didn't have no tight partner. Everybody was your partner then. We were new, and the old-timers weren't really talking. They wouldn't give us no kind of information. I would be asking as I was going along and I'd hear: "Keep your mouth shut! You know we don't talk out here. You just shut up and you walk and you follow, and don't get close to me; you just stay ten feet behind me. I've got two months left and I don't want one of you cherries getting my shit blown away. So just keep your damn mouth shut!" The guys was really strict like that. I mean, they meant it. These cats were pissed at being out in the field all the time, and when they got the ass, they got the ass at everybody. Not just the new guys, but the CO and anybody in the rear saying, "Why in the fuck did they send us out?" Maybe they thought that Alpha or Delta Companies got over on them by staying in the rear four days while they were there only two days. They had just a piss poor attitude in general. At night new guys would snore; so dudes would wake them up. And if they continued to snore, some dude would take a hand grenade and hold it in front of their face and say, and they meant it, man—"If you don't shut your mouth, and roll over on your side, we're all gonna die; but before that happens, I'm gonna stick this mouthful of apple down your throat. When I tell you to shut up that snoring, you shut up, man!" So these guys brought you along. But then I was starting to get pissed too, because these guys were talking to me like I was a dog, and I didn't want to be here anyway. I said, "Hey, man, just bug off." I was starting to talk back, getting into it. I couldn't get used to my pack and it was cutting the shit out of my shoulders. I was humping and swaying. And these guys were so neat, even though they looked like they got a lot more stuff than me, they were just humping along smooth as silk.

For a while we seemed to fall into a regular pattern of humping. Every Monday morning we'd have to take a big horse pill for malaria, which was hard to swallow. And every day we had to take a little yellow or white one. Then we'd take salt tablets all during the day because we'd be sweating like a dog. Every day we were moved by so many clicks (kilometers) through the brush on Search and Destroy missions. We'd be moving and cutting and moving and cutting our way through. We were moving from six o'clock in the morning till six o'clock in the evening. I don't care how many miles we walked, we never reached our destination till six. And wherever six o'clock caught us at, if it was a pretty good area, then the CO would call standdown right there, and we'd set up the perimeter. While we were setting up the perimeter, the CO would radio back to the command post and feed any information about where we were and how many kills we had that day back to TOC, back to the fire support base.

After a few weeks, we started going up the mountains. Other guys called them hills, but I called them mountains, man. Shit, I could look down and see the fucking clouds. We were just climbing and climbing and climbing. When I got to the top, wasn't nothing there. So I couldn't understand. I thought we were walking around in circles. I used to get pissed because it seemed to me we'd never be going any place. I questioned it, but I didn't ever say nothing to anyone directly. I would ask some of the guys that had been there a while, "Man, why the fuck we go up this hill, what we go up there for?" They'd say, "Charlie could be up there." We got up there and no Charlie, right? So down the hill into the valley we would go.

We were busting bush with machetes. We almost never got on trails. Once we got used to the company and started to learn a little, then the old-timers started to put the cherries—us new guys—out on point to cut through the brush. The only reason they didn't put us up there in the beginning was because they didn't want us to walk into an ambush. We didn't know the markings on trees, or maybe the three little pieces of wood on the ground that indicated a booby trap. The reason the Vietnamese would always mark it was to warn their own people. Just three little marks on a tree, barely visible, they could bypass the booby trap meant for us. Until we learned this, the old-timers wouldn't let us walk point or nothing like that. Half the time I would carry the M-16 and a bandolier with about twenty magazines, in addition to my pack. I was breaking into the routine pretty fast.

When I joined the company we were trying to deal with a hard-core division out of the North working in the same area. They were one number different from us; we were the 173d and they were the 174th out of North Vietnam. They were not only mutilating the dead, they were taking bamboo stakes and trimming them into spikes. When they killed you, they would mutilate you, and then they would take their unit patch and stick it on your forehead to let you know that they were the ones. Their patch had a reddish-yellow moon with four or five stars right above the moon. Everyone knew the 174th because they were gung ho; everyone remembered them for the simple reason that they really kicked ass. They were a well-disciplined unit. Later on we ran into them a number of times. So the guys were worried but only to the extent that we knew what had happened to other units that ran up against them. We felt that nobody could kick our ass. We felt tough and strong, because we had a unity and harmony that I don't think was matched in Vietnam by any other unit. In fact, we not only felt that the Vietnamese couldn't beat us, we felt sure there was no other American unit that could beat us if it came down to that. Maybe we were brainwashed, but we thought we was the best in the Nam. We knew that our unit was the first American ground fighting force in the Nam. We knew that we was the only unit that *jumped* into Nam. So we was pretty damn hardcore ourselves. We knew if we ever hooked up with the 174th — which we eventually did — we could take 'em. When we finally did, we lost a few wounded, but we counted some of their dead. We were told that their documents showed they were afraid of us. Now that I look back on it, the company commander was doing his job. But he used to hump us, man, until our bones ached. We would be wanting to stop and rest, stop and cook and eat, and he'd just hump us. Some days he'd hump us from can't see in the morning till can't see in the evening, and we'd be cursing and pissing at him. But I give him thanks, too, because I think if it wasn't for him driving us on in such a way, I might be dead right today. We called him Rabbit; he was the best CO I had in the Nam, and I had two others besides him. I never knew his real name. We called him Rabbit because he wasn't like the average CO walking through the jungle; he'd be running through the fucking jungle. But he was good, really sharp. Half the time we wanted to kill the bastard, and the other half of the time we loved him because he was that good. And he was fair.

You gotta have a fair CO. You got these chicken shit COs that hadn't been through any real combat. They'd be straight out of OCS with all this John Wayne bullshit. They'd come over and want to read out of the book on how it should go, man. You know, standard operating procedure. And their book would get you killed. When Rabbit was there, we dumped the book. You couldn't go by the book in Vietnam. Maybe in previous wars you could say, "We hide behind this," or, "We move over here, and this and that." But when you got a good company commander, he used his own discretion in certain situations. Lotta times the shit hit so fast, the book didn't help. It was constantly up to you to react in a certain way. If you reacted wrong, you were dead.

Take the L–shaped ambush. When you fell into that you knew right off where the major firepower was coming from. If you had a sharp company commander, he could take just one glance and tell what was happening. If you had one that got his face buried down in the fucking ground, soon as that shit started coming in, he was trying to hide from the heat, then your whole unit could get killed right there. Rabbit never got down on the ground. Half the time he was the only motherfucker up, checking things out. Where was the automatic weapons fire coming from? Where was the main body of the ambush? Then he would give you orders to move in—in the right direction! We knew that 95 percent of the people in the unit had total confidence in him; we knew that he could get us out of trouble. That confidence was very important. You had to remember that the company commander was only human. He could be out there for some bullshit purpose. As a captain, he was a career officer; he wanted to make rank. I've heard that there were company commanders in Vietnam that actually got fragged. They didn't give a damn about their men. When nightfall came and nobody could see, some grunt would take a hand grenade and just blow him away. It was that simple; hand grenades don't leave finger prints.

We had a lot of confidence in Rabbit. He was like the God-father. He was everything to us. His direction was our destination. Now, just cause he was the captain, people maybe felt they had to take orders from him. We didn't have to take orders from no fucking bastard. At least, I felt that way. He had a weapon; I had one too. We loved that guy and when he left us in the field, he made a little speech that was supposed to get us ready for the next company commander. He told us to drive on and stay strong, and remember the spirit of the people could move mountains. I guess in a way that affected us. We held on. Some of the guys are dead and gone and I loved 'em all. He tried to instill in us that there wasn't no black and white in Nam. You forgot about that shit. I felt that way, anyway.

It takes tragedy to bring people together. In our particular case, that tragedy brought us so close that I felt closer to everybody in that unit at the time than I do my own blood sisters and brothers. Because it was us. We'd seen hard times. We'd seen fear. It was THE family. I mean, it was us, man. It wasn't like a regular family that may not have enough food or jobs. In our particular family, we knew that in a few minutes everybody could be dead. We was close, without being "funny." I mean like gays. We was so close it was unreal. That was the first time in my life I saw that type of unity, and I haven't seen it since. And that was ten years ago. It was beautiful. It sort of chills you, brings goose bumps just to see it, just to feel it, cause the family is guys from all over the states, from New York and California, Chicago, Mississippi, 'Bama, everywhere. At first, you got all these funky types of personalities hooking up into one military unit. Everybody had their own little hatreds, their own little prejudices, biases. But after four, five, six months that disappeared. You just saw total unity and total harmony. It was really great, man. It was beautiful. That was the only thing that really turned me on in Vietnam. That was the only thing in Vietnam that had any meaning.

Stan

4 "THE PIG"*

Bob was probably somewhere in Vietnam by now, and I often wondered how he was making out. We continued the same routine in Bravo Company; nothing happening at all. All day long we'd walk around, then we'd set up camp at night, set out our claymore mines for protection. Night patrols were diminishing.

They started having reconnaissance teams that were trained to go on night patrols. We were not trained specifically for that. A lot of guys were getting wiped out because they didn't really know how to survive. We called the recon patrols "lurps." I guess when they had enough alerts in the country, all of a sudden orders came from high up, "No more night patrols." Man, we was happy as hell. So at night, when we set up our AO, we'd set up our claymore mines around the perimeter. It was about

*The M–60 machine gun, called "The Pig," was the firepower of the infantry company. The man that carried the pig was more vulnerable than the ordinary infantryman. At the same time, he was in the best position to protect the company until heavier support was available.

this time I moved over to 4th squad—Young's squad. So I had
to take orders from him. I didn't particularly like him. I just
didn't like the way he gave orders, maybe because he was from
the South.

One morning Young came back from meeting with the sergeants. He told us that we were to be walking about two or
three clicks. We were looking for an abandoned NVA training
ground, possibly another camp, really any evidence of VC or
NVA activities. That particular day we walked from about nine
o'clock that morning till about noon. I was sitting back, resting
on a log with my friend, Leon. The platoon sergeant came
around to Young. He said, "Hey, man, we got a VC tunnel over
here, you want to go?" Young jumped up, "Yeah, man, you
know I do. Hell, yes! Do I get to keep everything I find?" The
sergeant said, "Yeah, we'll think about it. But primarily we're
looking for maps, Young." Leon and I looked at each other—
"God damn fool," our look said. That was just what we thought
of the dude, anyway. Neither one of us liked the guy. We really
didn't have a tunnel rat. Some platoons did. I'd heard guys were
actually trained in the states to be tunnel rats. Apparently ours
had been wiped out or something. We weren't getting a new
supply, so Young and a few other guys were volunteering.
Young was tall, but he was skinny. That was why he could ease
in there. So we thought, "God damn fool," and our eyes followed him into the brush.

We went on sitting there talking about home, and then all of
a sudden there was a muffled "BOOM . . . " Everybody went
running. "Hey, man, get on the horn, man, call the medivac
chopper." I watched from a distance. I didn't go near the guys.
I didn't want to see them bring Young out. I guess I was shy
of seeing somebody blown to bits. Leon went on over there.
Word started getting around, "Young got it, man. Young got
hit by a booby trap."

In about five minutes a helicopter was there. Some guys went
down in the tunnel and pulled him out. He was blown apart,
but he was still alive and moaning. I think he was asking for his

mother. It was sad. I didn't like the guy, but I didn't want him to get blown away. I didn't want anybody to get blown away in this dirty ass war. This was the first casualty I'd witnessed since I'd been out in the boonies. I didn't want to see anybody mutilated. I didn't think I was ready to stomach it. So I just stayed behind. The CO got a radio report saying Young died on the way. Why in the shit did he go and volunteer for some bullshit like that? Just to get some trophy. The CO couldn't order anybody to go down inside a tunnel. At one time they could, but apparently there were complaints. So now he had to ask somebody if he wanted to go and they could always find some God damn idiot.

Carl, another buddy in the 4th squad came back over. Immediately Carl and I were saying, "Who's going to carry the pig?" Everybody knew the importance of the M-60, but not everybody could handle the weapon. Young had acquitted himself as a man that could handle the M-60. I didn't hear anybody indicating Young didn't know what to do, but I did hear a few guys say he used to cower behind the weapon. He was afraid of being hit, and he didn't really want to expose himself with the M-60.

I saw Young in a fire fight once. We were crossing this high bladegrass in a field. It must have been about two feet high. We were just crossing what looked as though it might have been barbed wire fence. And just then we got hit by three or four snipers. Everybody hit the ground. We thought somebody had gotten hit, but apparently a bullet had hit a guy's rucksack. The force of the bullet just threw him to the ground, and so he hollered out, "I'm hit." Everybody panicked. Young called for ammo. "God damn it, hurry and get that ammo up here," and he was shooting away, but we thought he was panicking. For a man that had been in the country as long as he had, he didn't look as though he were really stable with what he was doing. The platoon sergeant called, "Young up front. Young, Young, bring the pig up." Young looked at me. He started moving up, but his head was darting all around. Then he said, "OK, bring the God damn ammo." Carl and I came running low as we possibly could, following him up where the pig was. He was very, very nervous. When he would run out of ammo and start to reload, I noticed he was fumbling. That was when I first started wondering if this guy was really as competent with the weapon as he should be. Our platoon CO had apparently called in a couple of Puff the Magic Dragons.* They came in and zapped the treeline, and the firing stopped.

The sergeant came over and got on Young's ass. And this sergeant was from North Carolina, too. He just cut the guy up right there. "Young, I don't know what the fuck's wrong with you, but you're not fast enough with that God damn pig, I know that. You ass around too God damn much." Then he walked off leaving Young trying to give an explanation. Carl and I looked at each other but didn't say anything, because we didn't know how to handle the pig.

The pig belonged to the guy with experience, the guy who could keep cool in a fire fight, a guy that knew what he was doing, and not to a guy that was green. It was the only major firepower in our entire platoon. Your automatic weapons' fire was your heavy artillery; the pig had greater range. It was your heavy heavy. If a man panicked and really didn't know how to handle the heavy heavy, you really didn't have too much. A lot of guys didn't want to carry it because it was very heavy and it was lethal—meaning it was lethal to both you and to Charlie. Obviously, Charlie tried to knock you out first. They tried to hit you with RPGs.** Their first target of interest was the man with the machine gun. If they knocked out that machine gun, they could easily overrun the platoon. Then the only thing they had to contend with was just light weapons. In a heavy fire fight, when you got a man that really didn't know how to handle the pig, the sergeant would end up firing it.

Young had been the M-60 man. Now who was going to carry

*Puff the Magic Dragons were old converted Air Force aircraft like the C-47 (DC-3).
**Soviet-designed rockets.

the pig? I said to Carl, "Hell, you can have it, you've got seniority." Carl said, "Shit, I don't want that God damn thing."
I said, "Well, hell, I don't want it either." "Shit, man, you're
a whole lot bigger than me." "Why, shit, you got the seniority,
you been in-country a month longer than I have." "Oh, man,
fuck it," he said, "there's only the two of us left." "I know it."
It was only a three-man squad. That was how low our company had gotten. I think our company was only running sixty
or seventy men. Our platoon was no more than twenty guys
now. Sergeant Doherty was a platoon sergeant at that time. He
was from North Carolina, or some God damn place like that.
But he was good in a fire fight and that was all that really
counted. Either you were good in a fire fight or you were a
coward. That was all there was to it. That was how Doherty
made E-5. So anyway, Doherty came over. He had Young's pig
in his hand. He was shaking his head. He was really shook up
about it, because he liked Young. They were buddies. They
were both from the South. "All right, who gets the pig?" I said,
"Well, hell, don't look at me." "Some God damn guy is going to
carry the pig. Now, it's Young's pig, he's gone and you know it,
so I gotta give the pig to someone. Carl, you take the pig, you've
got seniority." So Carl had the pig. He was a little guy. He
weighed only about 130 pounds soaking wet, and here I was,
I probably weighed 185. But I didn't say anything. At first Carl
didn't say anything either. Then he said, "Well, set the God
damn thing down." He didn't even take it. Doherty said, "Well,
take it." "God damn it, I got it. You've already assigned it to
me — now set the fucker down. I'll pick it up." Doherty set the
pig on the ground right beside Carl. I didn't laugh. I knew he
was serious. Anyway, Carl was the pig man.

In a short time we moved out. Everybody was kind of quiet
because Young had got it. No matter if a certain group of guys
didn't like him, he was still a man that just got blown away.
You know, it just brought us back to hard-core reality. This
was a war; this was not any bullshit. When you didn't get hit
for so many days, you started bullshitting a lot, you started
forgetting that you were in the boonies fighting a war.

Carl was having a hell of a time with the pig. He had it slumped all over. I thought, God, man, if we got hit, this motherfucker didn't have Jack shit together. Firepower was firepower, and here we had a guy that probably didn't know what the fuck to do with it if we did get hit. The gun might have been pointed down toward the God damn ground. If he'd walked by a branch, hit it, and the gun went this way, away he went — the M-60 weighs about twenty-four pounds. But it was not really that heavy once you got used to it. I knew I was going to have to end up getting this God damn thing. I knew that I was. But I tried to put it off. I knew that it was inevitable, because I wasn't safe with this guy. I guess all this training started coming to my mind. And I thought how important the weapon was. There was only two of us in this squad, just him and me. We hadn't been getting hit, but I started thinking, well, I was bigger than this guy. I could handle this weapon better than he could. And nobody else wanted to volunteer for the pig. Somebody had to carry it. The rest of the guys didn't want to carry it, because, as I said before, it was the weapon that Charlie aimed for . . .

I guess the guys had been psyching me out for it, anyway. Apparently they felt I would be able to handle the weapon. I knew the brothers were talking. "Man, we don't have anybody that can really put out any firepower. Ever since Matthew Griffin went in to the rear, we don't have anybody that we have any confidence in in this whole God damn platoon." They were talking about it at night as we came in. So they were looking at me like, "Hey, man, why don't you carry the damn thing?"

One day Carl and I were walking along in a stream. Carl had the pig, and it fell into the water while he was trying to walk; the weapon went one way and he went another. I think he knew I was checking him out. I think he thought to himself, "Overboard with it." And so I said, "Hey, Carl, lemme have that God damn gun, man."

"You want it, man? Here . . . "

"Yeah, Carl, lemme try to get it cleaned up. I know it hasn't been cleaned in I don't know when. Probably won't even fire."

"Oh, man, I thought you'd never ask!" He really started painting a beautiful picture about me having the weapon. "You know, I can fire it, man, but I know you can handle it a lot better; you're stronger than I am," and shit like that, anything to have me keep the damn thing.

Anyhow, that's how I ended up with the pig. It was no problem with me. I started really liking the weapon. It made me feel powerful to have it.

The sergeant saw that I was really interested in it, because I used to keep it cleaned all the time. When it seemed like we weren't running up on anything, he used to set up a target practice, let me take it out and shoot it. I never saw him take time to do that with anybody else. He taught me how to really maneuver the weapon, how to aim down the sights and keep the lead going straight, how to fire effectively. The fault of a lot of guys with the M-60 and the reason why they used to get wiped out was because they would fire the M-60 wildly. Like Young was doing that day, clips flying all over the place. He had his eyes shut, just pulling the trigger. Shit, the lead was all going up in the God damn treetops. Charlie was just sitting right down there on the ground waiting to beam our ass. So I kept the forearm weight on it to hold it level. I took aim through the big sight right on the end of the barrel. I had to ignore the vibration, watch the sight, keep it leveled downward. I used to keep it leveled at where a man's waist would be. That was how I would decipher how low I was going to shoot it. If I thought a man was up in the treetops, I'd level it right where I thought that treetop was, and I'd shoot down just about a foot below that, and I would be lethal. I'd blow the guy out of there.

When I saw the sergeant was really taking an interest in me, I asked him all kinds of questions about the weapon. He taught me how to fire on the run, in a crouch position, laying on my back, falling down, anyway I wanted to. He just told me all kinds of tricks about firing this weapon. He was a brand new platoon sergeant; one of those smart guys. He hadn't been in the boonies long himself, maybe about a month. He was from the South, too, but a different sort of a southern guy. Didn't seem as though he was a working class southern guy, more like a career soldier. Had to be to come from the states an E–6. Figured he might have come out of one of those special NCO schools that I mentioned earlier. He knew his shit, mechanically. Maybe he was an M–60 specialist. I didn't know. The guy knew the weapon, though. I got that information from him, and after that, I developed a reputation very, very fast. The guys started getting confidence in me.

One afternoon we were in mountainous terrain with a lot of streams. We were looking for an NVA unit. We saw a big grass fire on the side of the mountain. At first we didn't know who started the fire or what was happening up there. We just knew that we were chasing part of an NVA regiment that was on the run. By the time we climbed all the way up this big hill, the fire had burned out and we just found a whole hill charred to nothing. We were going up to help out Echo Company. Charlie tried to freak us out. He had set fire to this hill so we couldn't find him, since we wouldn't be able to see through all this smoke. We did a lot of forced marching to get to this God damn hill, and we got to nothing. That used to happen sometimes. We'd be running, running, supposedly to help some company out, and by the time we got there, nothing was there. It used to really give a lot of guys the ass.

We spent the night in those hills. We were going to keep looking for that NVA unit. But we could never find them. We'd get close on their trail. We'd think we were getting hot, very close to them, and we'd start walking fast, but still we couldn't find them. They'd just disappear.

Still in this mountainous terrain, Hardcore Castile was walking point. All of a sudden we heard rapid fire. We all hit the dirt and stayed down there waiting for something else to happen. Then we heard some more fire, and someone up ahead yelled that Hardcore had wiped out three NVA soldiers. They were sitting in the trail frying their fish for lunch. Hardcore walked right up and wiped them out. Some guys went off looking for another NVA. They ran him for a mile or two, but he disappeared totally. That same day, in the same area, Hardcore's squad found a hootch full of rice, just tons of rice. Apparently it was quite common for the VC to have the peasants deliver rice to an area for the NVA to pick up. These guys Hardcore wiped out were a squad that was probably sent up to guard it until the main NVA units came through.

The very next day we were walking along inside of this streambed, just about to cross. I had my pig at the ready because of all the previous activity. As of yet, I had not really been in a fire fight with the pig. We felt that we were going to get hit. That's why we were walking in the stream. We didn't want to walk in the upper jungle area where it was real thick. We liked our CO; he was smart. I started understanding why he always had us walking out in the open. Shit, I didn't blame him. I'd rather be walking out in the open than walking through the brush and getting ambushed. In the brush, we couldn't see a God damn thing. We were vulnerable everywhere, but in the open we could see to move and dive. We couldn't dive anywhere if we were in the brush. Anyway, as I was walking across this stream, all hell broke loose. We got hit.

I hit the water with Carl beside me. That was the first fire fight we had been in and we worked like a precision team. Carl threw his rucksack off his back as he hit the ground. I was firing as I hit the ground. You know, firing right up at the brush where I thought their firepower was coming from. This was in the broad afternoon, so we were not going to see anything, not that close, because Charlie didn't have to be ten yards away to eat us up with an AK-47. I fired all my ammo up instantaneously, but Carl was right there. He was clipping ammo onto the belts as if it was going up and into the slot on top of the pig, just that quick. I knew then that we would make a hell of a team. I fired and fired that pig. I never did let go. Guys were yelling, "Goff, Goff, over there," pointing out where they thought the fire was coming from, and I was eating that pig up. Wherever they were pointing, I was laying it in there.

Apparently I was laying it up there so heavy and so hard that we never did get any retaliation. By the way, the pig flew apart that afternoon. They commonly did that, especially if you were one of these guys that was really not afraid to fire them. When you were really blowing lead in there, you were supposed to let it cool off every now and then. When you were like me, man, I figured, fuck the God damn pig—fire this God damn thing. That was what it was made for. So what happened was that after firing for about twenty minutes, the bolt started popping right out of the side of it. Then the barrel screwed up. It went forward and sort of slipped partly off by itself. But Carl had an extra barrel and he brought it to me. I was lying in the water, and I threw one off and put the other one on, and started firing again. Then the pin came out of the God damn thing. Carl and I started laughing. I didn't let up off that trigger for about twenty-five minutes nonstop—that was a long time, really. When you fired it so long, it got you all jittery inside. It was like guys that work jackhammers. After a while, if you don't stop, it has your nerves completely like jelly inside. That's the way the pig does you.

After the fire fight, Sergeant Doherty walked up and said, "Hey, Goff, you did a hell of a good job, man. You did a God damn good job, laying that lead down." I found out two guys got hurt in our small company. Doherty got hit in the leg, so he was limping. It was just a flesh wound, but he went in on that. I was like a new man to the guys. I mean, they had respect for me as an individual that could really handle the pig. The NVA just disappeared. No body count. The guys went up in the brush looking for them. I stayed down with the pig to protect the unit. But nobody saw anything at all. It was probably a handful of guys, maybe three or four. This was the first real heavy fire fight I actually got into, where guys got hurt. Before, it was just snipers who harassed us. Actually, it was really a light fire fight —thirty minutes. That was nothing compared to the battle that was coming up that lasted for three hours. But I didn't know that then.

The CO called us in to get the medivac. All the rest of the guys chopped out an AO. That was one thing about a gun squad. We really didn't have to do too much, except maintain our weapons and guard duty. Along with the guys that got hurt, the chopper took the weapon in. I was going to get another M-60 that same afternoon. I got an M-16 in the meantime. We weren't going to leave out of the area, because a handful of NVA might have meant larger units around. The CO reported the fire fight and headquarters sent in helicopters to search the area. In no time the helicopters were all over trying to find them. But Charlie was gone. He didn't want no part of that shit. So we finally moved off into another area to chow down. And later that afternoon out came another weapon. They sent out another barrel, too. So I had another M-60; it was practically new, very tight—a damn good weapon. It was in much better shape than the first one. And that was the one I kept throughout my stay in the boonies.

Then we heard that we were going to get resupplied, so we walked back to LZ Ross just like before. Carl and I were assigned this one bunker and we looked at it. I said, "Oh, man, shit, we got to carry sandbags and reinforce this damn thing . . ."

Bob

5 ANOTHER TRIP WITH THE M-60

I didn't know that Stan, too, had gotten the pig. In my second month in the field the CO gave it to me. Back at Fort Lewis in the qualifying tests with the M–60, I'd shot the best in the division, and I had a paper for that. They had all my records in Vietnam. I didn't really want any part of the M–60, but they wanted a good man to carry the pig. Some of the old–timers were getting short. One of 'em, a guy named Charles something, was carrying the pig. He was about ready to ship. He was from North Carolina, and he was supposed to be the best pig man on the flanks. In a heavy weapons' platoon, one pig watched the front and the other covered the flanks. Anyway, they started looking around for one of the cherries that was qualified to carry it; I hadn't been there long, but I was qualified. They didn't go through any ceremony with it. They just said, "Here, you carry this motherfucking pig!"

No one wanted it. The pig position was the one attacked by the enemy after the company commander and the radio man. If they could, they wanted to take out the machine gun because

that was where the firepower was coming from. Everybody
knew that, even in training. So I humped it. First thing was that
I had to get used to the extra twenty-four pounds. Once you
were humping, the pig man was more likely to get hung up in
the brush. Everybody got hung up, but the pig barrel is long
and the weapon is bulkier. You were carrying tripods, too. The
weapon has so many different side pieces that it was easy to get
hung up. It was tucked under your arm in the ready position
with the strap for support across your neck. You were going
through all that brush and you can't imagine how thick it was.
Except for the Vietnamese, my main foe was the wait-a-minute
vines. I could be walking along, and, all of a sudden, the vine
took the gun from me. I was tearing at the vine, trying to kick it,
and it was raining. I was wet, and I was mad. One time I was
walking along and the vine completely pulled the gun out
of my hand, and the barrel stuck in the mud. I had to clean it.
There were days like that. Anyway, old-timers didn't want no
part of that gun, but they wanted someone on it who could use
it.

Some guys in a fire fight froze. You never knew until the
actual fire fight the effect on a person. In my first fire fight, we
had about six or seven guys just get down, man. I mean, they
just weren't throwing out any firepower—and we were only
under sporadic fire. It wasn't nothing heavy, just minor hit-
and-run stuff. I guess maybe eight or nine VC decided to welcome me to the Nam. In that fire fight, when I saw guys that
froze, I knew right then who was who. You knew who was up
there firing with you. That was where my tight partners came
in. I knew who could stand and fight and who wouldn't. We
didn't say nothing. These were guys to keep our eyes on. For
instance, if we got hit by heavy shit, I wouldn't rely on these
guys too much. I might have been firing to cover my area, but
I would be watching their area as well. All Charlie needed was
one opening and he would take advantage of it. He could tell
where he was getting fire from. Naturally, he was going to try
to find the hole in the defense. That put more of a burden on us,

but a little later, some guys began to function a little better. In fact, we got these guys off to the side and threatened them somewhat: "Hey, man, if you don't put down no fucking firepower and I get hit, or one of my partners, then we may turn around and put some smoke on your ass." We told 'em, "If you're not throwing out firepower, you gonna get killed anyway, because Charlie gonna come right over your position and shoot you in the fucking head. You might as well get up and try to run him back off." We just gave them an ultimatum. That helped us begin to develop as a unit. After that little talk, it didn't take too long. They saw the logic of it.

No one took any chances in the bush. Everytime something jumped, they fired it up. The Vietnamese had what was called an L-shaped ambush. They waited until they got the main body of troops in the killing zone. I don't care how many people —there used to be about 120 of us—everybody in the killing zone was supposed to be dead in approximately seven to ten seconds, if the ambush was effective. That was why it was very important to have that point man stay alert, for the simple reason that he was the first man in the woods. The people behind him couldn't see what was happening because the bush was so thick; people in back of the point were concentrating on the flanks and watching for booby traps. But the point man was the first man through the woods, so he might have picked up a little noise or some other clue to let him know that there might be an ambush up ahead. A lotta times we used to have scout dogs, and the dogs would alert the point, cause they could smell out the Viet Cong and North Vietnamese. Then the point of the platoon would simply raise his hands with his palms up to the man right behind him. Everyone would halt and the word would get back to the company commander. Everyone stopped, and each person would start alternating on the flanks; one man would face to the right, and one man would face to the left, automatically.

The ambushes were set up to annihilate you, just dust you in a hurry. The trick in an ambush was to attack the main body.

If you didn't know where that last man was, then you didn't know how many people you were up against. Say you hit the point man, you still didn't know how long the column was. You might have been hitting a battalion. And everybody in that column was going to just come right on over your ass on the ambush site. But if you saw the last man come through, then you knew you could get a full count. It was proven that some units hit too soon. Sometimes you had to wait a couple of extra seconds just to make sure that that was the last man because they might have had two units running. That last man might have been maybe twenty-five feet from the beginning of the new column. That was the nerve-wracking part of the ambush. You were about ten feet off the trail; everything was camouflaged, even your face. You had a bush over your head or maybe you were lying flat. You could actually count people as they came by. Once the last man was through, that was when the shorter part of the L-shaped ambush opened up; that was the signal for everybody to pop up. Usually the claymores went off first, then frags, and then the smoke—rifle platoons started raking the area. The claymore mines disorganized them because the mines were so effective. Much more effective than taking a shot with your weapon, cause it was going to clear out the whole area for sixty feet in front of you. The claymores were set up along the long part of the "L" and you might even have doubled up. When the claymores went, that was the first indication that everyone should have been operating.

Each side set up ambushes. Sometimes it took up to a week to set up an effective one. An ambush could be set up and then a unit go off course; maybe just enough for the ambush to not be too effective. Our CO (or theirs) would call the ambush off.

We used to run out patrols every day—that was what was called Lurps. Five-man teams that would go out and analyze the enemy movements, try to pick up some inside information. They were strictly a scouting force. They had interpreters, and the reason they moved in such a small group was for noise discipline. The smaller the group was, the more effective it

could be. When you got 120 guys moving through the brush,
you got guys getting pissed and cursing; we used to hump D-
handled shovels and they'd be banging off trees. With that
many people they could hear us coming miles away.

When you were caught in an L-shaped ambush, the main
thing was not to panic. I know it's easy to say, "Don't panic,"
but out in the bush, like I say, if you hesitated, that was it.
There's two kinds of fighters—the quick and the dead. When
you got in that kind of situation, there was only one thing to
do. You had to charge that ambush. You had to go right over
them to get out of the killing zone. After you walked into the L,
that was the only way out. The L was set up so they weren't
on either side of the trail—else they'd be shooting each other.
So they planted pungi sticks on each side of the trail. You
couldn't fall down on the trail or else you'd be falling right into
death. And if you froze and didn't know what to do, that gave
them more time to fire you up in the killing zone. You couldn't
go back—120 men couldn't turn around so you had to go right at
the direction the fire was coming from. They were faced then
with 120 men coming at them. But they'd been following you;
whatever it took, they had it. If you were a company, maybe
they were a battalion. If they were going to take on a company,
they were going to have personnel to deal with that. If they got
a battalion-sized force, it might have been strung out eight
blocks long to meet your company-sized two-block force.
Right in back of the ambush, they would build bunkers. If they
had to pull back, they withdrew behind the bunkers, and then
the bunkers opened up to stop your force from overrunning
them because you blew their ambush.

Usually, if you got attacked, it was because you got caught in
an ambush or you ran up on them by accident. Eventually, if
you got through, you were gonna hit a base camp. This was
where they were consolidated. They had fortified bunkers and
tunnels that ran for a mile or more. When the Phantom jets and
the chopper gunships came in, they wanted to have an escape
route. If you beat back their assault and started a counter-

attack, they could escape underground. Especially if there was napalm. Napalm takes all the oxygen out of the air. White phosphorous can't be put out so when they got hit, they went underground. They knew when the attack started that air power was on the way.

We had an FO (Forward Observer) traveling with us; when we made contact, he'd automatically call in some heat on them. Even after we got artillery support, he'd call in Phantoms. We'd pop smoke to tell the Phantom where we were at. The FO would call in the grid coordinates to tell the plane where we felt they were at. Then we'd call out a marker round. If that round was where we wanted it, then we would ask for so much HE (High Explosive). We always had that, though sometimes, if the NVA were in too close, we couldn't call in nothing. Then we just got to beat back the assault if we could. We tried to make sure that Charlie was not on ridges above us. If we figured we could handle them, we didn't want that stuff too close because the shrapnel would hit us. But we wanted it close enough so it took care of some of them; then we figured that we'd take care of the rest. Then the gun ships started coming. They could do a closer inspection from above. They circled. Maybe two to four Cobras. They just circled around looking. They were constantly firing rockets and mini-guns. Oh, man, there was so much firepower, they tore up the place.

The first few months, we worked the area around Bao Loc. We humped up along the hillsides and all through the swamp lands. We patrolled the mountain right next to the village at Bao Loc. But we'd be from thirty to forty miles away. We'd be out maybe eighty days at a time. We'd run into sporadic contact. Sometimes we'd get into a firefight, not a real big one, but it was big enough that people were getting killed. The company commander figured out that the NVA and VC were coming down from the Dalat area into the Bao Loc area, raiding villages and killing people. Their strength was in the mountains, and we headed up there eventually. In the meantime, we were wading through the swamps, making contact here and there. We also worked the tea plantation which was about twenty miles back from Bao Loc.

The swamp was the shits, man. It was dense with muck and black water and millions of leeches. The foliage was so dense and so tight, the sun couldn't get in and I'd be thinking I might see a dinosaur come running through there. And plants—you never seen them grow that big. Some plants would get as big as a regular yard tree. We saw a lizard on a tree that looked like an alligator. Everything was tropical and seemed prehistoric. And mosquitos constantly, all over the place. Then we had to be on the lookout for snakes. We might come out on a little dry parcel of land into a heavy bamboo area. Then we would worry about the bamboo viper. Charlie would hide out in the bamboo. He'd cut out a little square area and have him a little house there. You couldn't detect it from a spotter plane. He'd grow his corn and rice right in that area, so he wouldn't need much re-supply. He'd have hootches made out of straw and bamboo. To get to these dry areas where there was VC, guys would get stuck in the swamp up to their waist. By the time the last guy came through, the mud and muck was getting deeper and deeper.

It was during that time in the swamps that the monsoon set in. We were just rain wet all the time. We went to bed on the ground wet. We had an air mattress, but that lasted one day. Even if we didn't puncture it that first night, we'd be so tired the next day we wouldn't want to blow it up. In fact, I traded some of my beans to a guy so he would inflate it. A few guys went for that, but after a while they said, "Fuck it, man, I ain't blowin' nothin' up." Once we logged in, made camp, what we tried to do was clean an area. We were trying to cut brush, but we got little stubs from the brush we cut sticking up because we couldn't dig down and get all the roots out. So as soon as we laid our air mattresses down, they became ground mattresses. The little stubs stuck right through the damn things. That was why most guys just threw them away after a while. Actually, they'd tear them up because we didn't want to leave nothing for the enemy. We was told we weren't supposed to leave anything on the trails; the Vietnamese would take all the tin cans from the C-rations and make them into shrapnel. He would take gunpowder and pack it tightly; he'd compress nails and broken glass and stuff like that into a tin can. The next thing we knew, he'd got something better than our hand grenades. So we didn't want to leave nothing like that out there.

Like I said, I hated that monsoon; I hated the leeches. I hated the idea of just being out there for so long. Forget about showers or baths. Hell, only way I'd take a wash up was whenever I came to a stream that wasn't too swampy. Then I'd jump off in there and kinda wash my body up. I'd been used to hygiene and keeping myself clean. But after awhile, I just forgot about that. I stayed dirty, and muddy. The mud dried, then I was right back into the rice paddies. I was funky. I mean, I stunk, man, I really stunk. It was something to aggravate us all the time. We were harassed by mosquitos and leeches, the monsoon, and all the strenuous movement. We were always moving. There was not a day went by that we thought, "Hey, we're going to take a break, going to take a rest, today's a holiday." There was no holiday in the Nam. After a while I didn't give a shit what day it was. All I was thinking was how glad I'd be when stand down came at night. When we got wherever we were going, I could put my body down for a minute.

We was making contact almost every night. I was scared of every little lightning bug or anything that moved. I thought it was a VC. In the day I was all right. At night anything could happen. The CO would designate which guys would take their turn on night ambush, which could get kind of hairy. The purpose of the night ambush was so we wouldn't get ambushed ourselves. If, for instance, we had made contact that day and we had so many kills, then we knew Charlie had got his ass kicked. Could have been his brother or some friend got killed that day. So we had to go back down the trail knowing he was following us. We went with maybe eight or ten people and were thinking about gettin' hit. When we went on ambush, we would go back down the trail about a half–a–mile. Then we'd get off the side of the trail about fifteen feet, set up claymore mines, and in some cases we'd set trip flare wires across the trail. When they hit the trip flare wires, right then and there they'd be in our killing zone. We'd just pop the claymores which would spray an area about sixty feet straight out in front and about forty feet in width to the sides. That could be hairy, too. If the first part of the enemy was coming up the trail and they hit the trip wire and we hit them, they might have been only the point of a whole regiment. It was doubly hard to tell at night—it was pitch black. If that happened, we were in trouble. They were going to come and get our ass. But ambushes were standard operating procedure, something we had to do every night, whether it was raining or not. We would have a radio man with us. And at night, to keep noise discipline, we would put the radio on squelch. This meant no one could talk to us. The CO couldn't come in and say, "OK, how's it going down the trail there?" Usually we would get a couple of clicks, like "bomp, bomp" to let you know that the CO wanted to get you on the horn, that he had something to tell you. Then you'd have to get down and whisper. You had to be as quiet as possible. The next morning we'd contact the CO. He'd say, "OK, come on back in," and we'd tell him which way we was coming back in and our estimated time of arrival. We'd have to take up our trip flare wires and claymore mines. We would put out our own LP (Listening Post) while we're taking up the wires. Then we'd scurry on back into camp. Once we got in, we would chow down. The CO would have OPs (Observation Posts) and LPs out with security set up on the flanks. After we ate, it was time to hump again.

When guys came in from night ambush, they had to get their shit together and get that rucksack ready to hump. At "stand–to" everybody was up, helmets on and facing outward. The company commander, first sergeant and all the platoon leaders would meet in the center of this circle of grunts kind of like a wagon train. They'd chart out the day's movement while we were on alert. It took about half–an–hour, maybe forty–five minutes to make sure everybody had their orders correct on what to do in case we got hit. They were looking at a map of the terrain: where was a possible ambush site? While you were standing on standto, you might open a can with a P–38 opener and just reach on down, jack. Otherwise, you would just eat as you walked. Lotta guys wouldn't be hungry. When they had a little time, and felt like it, they might cook something up. There was no breakfast. Shit. Sometimes guys would take their canteen cup—a kind of multiple use thing—and make hot cocoa with these little instant bags. Some guys in the rear ripped off claymore mines and took out the composition B or C–4. It was better than a blowtorch. You'd take a little piece about an inch long. Then you'd take a little C–ration can and cut it around on both ends with a beer opener and make a few holes in the side. That was your stove. You just set that on the ground and dropped in that composition B, took a match, and hit it one time. Whooff! Put your cup right on top, and in about two seconds you got yourself a treat. Everybody kept their can, and that was what a lotta guys used to argue about: "Hey, which one of you motherfuckers stole my stove?" But a lotta times you wouldn't have time to cook. So you just ate right outta the can. The heat would make the food you were carrying warm. So when you got back from night ambush, you got just enough time to get your rucksack ready, completely compact again so your frags wouldn't be dropping as you went. Then you grabbed a bite to eat and it was time to get on.

At that time, our main purpose was to look for caches—guns, rice, corn, ammo, any type of thing that would supply the Vietnamese and keep them strong. They would hide it in tunnels and caves. Sometimes they'd have enough guns and rice to supply a whole division for a year. They would have it buried and we would have to find it and destroy it—or we used to have the Chinooks (we called them "shithooks") airlift it out.

Sometimes we'd have to cut out a landing zone if, for instance, another one of the companies got hit. It didn't matter how far away — maybe forty or fifty miles, maybe only ten. First thing the CO did was call all the platoon leaders together for another poop meeting. It was a change of plans meeting because somebody got hit, and we learned that they were sending choppers out to take us to where the heat was to give them other guys support. After the poop meeting, all the platoon leaders came back to give their guys the rundown. Then the CO ran out so many elements into the bush for observation and listening, so we wouldn't be surprised while we were cutting out a new landing zone. We humped chain saws; they got the job done in a hurry. They made a lotta noise, but then we were leaving out of that area anyway. Whenever we'd get resupplied, and we was in a thick area, we'd use the chain saws, and that was a thing that used to bug me — when we'd use the chain saw and we were gonna continue to stay there. You know that every VC and his mother knew you were there, if they didn't before.

We didn't have much time to get the LZ ready before the choppers would come and start lifting out parts of our company. Each chopper would take out six guys — three on each door. If the LZ where we were going was hot, the first chopper would pop red smoke. The first guys out were the first guys in. Even if we didn't get the red smoke, we'd fire up the landing zone anyway as a precaution. The door gunners would just rake the whole area as they were coming in. Sometimes I would be going in with the first few choppers, sometimes the last few.

When you got in first, it was always a shaky situation, because you knew that you didn't have that much help in case you got hit. As you were coming in to the new landing zone, you checked out for pungi sticks. Even if you were firing at the tree line, you still had to give the CO the information on the situation at the landing zone. The radio man relayed the message so they knew what to expect. A few times the bulk of the company was moved with Chinooks. Once you get on the landing zone, you faced out toward the bush or wherever the firing was coming from. You'd start assaulting the bush, and as soon as you had chased the enemy away from the treeline, then you automatically assumed their position. You would secure all around the landing zone in a big circle. When the whole company was finally in the LZ, then you started to move out in the direction the company commander designated.

You were really scared all the time. You never did get completely used to it, but you learned to handle it. As you learned the tactics, you became more familiar with the situation and this reassured you. But you never became complacent. Changes in the terrain could unsettle you. The terrain was funny. You climbed these hills in a big radius around Bao Loc, and then you went down through gorges into valleys. This area was really swamp land; it was very dense with lots of heavy foliage. There were lots of leeches, malaria–carrying mosquitos, snakes; it was a rough area to go through. You were constantly up and down from hills into swamps.

We were doing this kind of operation when B Company got hit. Actually, we had just come to the rear after being out there in the swamps and hills for about eighty days. B Company had been hit pretty bad. They had got ambushed and a whole platoon had been killed, just mutilated. So our CO told us, "OK, fellows, put it on; we're going back out." We were supposed to be in the rear for a four–day rest, but we had been there for about a day when we got the news. So we went back out to give B Company some support. We started tracking the Vietnamese who had wiped out B Company. Finally we came down into this valley to a tea plantation, one of the old French types. There was a village nearby and we asked them questions, trying to find out if they had seen this unit that had destroyed B Company. Had they come across anyone like that? But we couldn't get any information from them. That night we went out on a night field operation. On a night march it was almost impossible to see where you were going; it was pitch black. You were making all kinds of noise. Everybody in the world knew you were coming. The CO split the company in half. I guess we was a couple of miles out from where we left the other half of the company. We heard all this firing from where we had come, so we started back. By the time we got there, our fire fight was over. We found out that the ARVNs, our allies that were supposed to be there to support us, had run out and left the rest of the company to fight alone. All our people there was messed up. The guys that weren't dead, or just about dead, were wounded.

The next morning we started tracking this Vietnamese unit into the hills, making heavy contact in the woodlines. We started closing in. These guys were running. They would stop and dig in for a day or two, just to fight us off. They wanted to try to slow us up because we were too tight on them. We had quite a few companies working in the same area, so they stopped and fought, and then they would slip away again.

It was about this time that I stepped on a pungi stick. I got that off the landing zone. This whole landing zone was loaded with pungis. At first I didn't come out of the field for it. I kept humping and the field medic took care of it. It happened a second time when we went to help Bravo Company. Alpha was down the hill in the same AO catching hell. As we were coming in on the LZ, we saw the first chopper couldn't land. Vietnamese in the treelines were firing the fucker up; I mean just tearing the blades right off the chopper. So they had to pull out and keep trucking. I was in the third chopper. There was a chopper in front of us and a chopper behind us. I want you to picture this. We were coming into the landing zone, and the helicopter just swooped down maybe ten feet off the ground, maybe a little higher, fifteen feet off the ground. As it got that close to the ground, you gotta jump off, cause he was boogying out of there. They didn't want to lose a chopper, right? So we jumped as we saw fire coming from the bush. We knew what to expect before we got there. The first chopper had popped red smoke and taken his guys on out. Eventually he would put them on another chopper back in the rear or try to make it in again if the chopper wasn't damaged too bad. In the meantime, the Vietnamese had opened up on the second chopper. The door gunners on each side of my chopper were kicking ass behind their mounted M-60 machine guns. They kept firing as we

came down. As we started to jump out of the chopper, I could
see that we were catching hell, too. Shit flying all around our
heads. I jumped and as soon as I hit the ground, I could feel
something pierce the jungle boot. The fucking pungi stick was
stuck about an inch up in there. Man, there was a sharp pain,
but I was running like a motherfucker. I was dragging that
damn pungi stick with me because it was stuck in the boot.
Other guys were hollering and yelling that they were being hit.
A whole bunch of guys got the same thing. The whole LZ was
saturated with pungi sticks set up at forty-five degree angles
facing each other. They were sticking up in all directions all
over the place. Charlie was in the treeline surrounding the
whole LZ. If you hit the ground, you landed on a pungi stick;
if you stood up, you got shot. Coming into the LZ, I was concentrating on the treeline. I couldn't see that there were pungi
sticks in the LZ. It just looked like a clearing in the trees where
the elephant grass was growing. When I landed in the elephant
grass, which was about two or three feet high, it seemed like
I had got some cover. The pungi sticks changed all that.

  In that situation, all we could do was hit the treeline. In other
words, we ran directly into the firing like crazy, throwing frags,
trying to hit them every way we could. We couldn't stay on the
LZ; we had to get out of it. Everybody was exposed. The company commander was going crazy. He was yelling, "Get the
fuck to the treeline, get them bastards outa there." They didn't
back up; we pushed them hard, put a little smoke on their ass;
they had to leave. So we fucked them up, man. We didn't get
but a couple of deads out of it. They was well concealed, but
finally they had to jump and run. And we did it ourselves. No
air support. That was why airborne got the Air Medal after
twenty-five combat assaults. In a combat assault, we was the
support. Anyway, we ran them on back up in the hills. But we
didn't go too far, just far enough to secure the LZ so we could
get our main force in there. Remember now, they wasn't running out but six choppers at a time. With three dudes in each
door we had no more than about thirty-six people out there

and that was all. And we didn't know how big a force we was running into. Maybe ten minutes later—I'm not sure, I wasn't paying no attention to time—the other choppers started coming in. We were still trying to secure the LZ. Some of the other guys were getting fire from the opposite side. We worked our side of the bush with the few minutes we had. When more choppers came in, they started chasing around over that way. By this time, the company commander was on the radio telling these guys in the choppers what to expect when they came into the landing zones: "Watch out for the pungi sticks!" Finally, when the shit died down somewhat, the medics started to evacuate people and check out the guys that could go on.

A couple of guys got hit. We laid them down and the medics were working on them. That was why they couldn't get to us. I wouldn't say that a pungi stick was minor, but it wasn't so serious. More choppers came in and took out the wounded. Pretty soon the medic got around to me and a few other fellows. He tried to get out all the shit and poison from the wound.

Charlie put feces on the pungi stick in order to cause infection. And because it was hot and humid, your whole fucking leg could swell up in a matter of hours. A pungi wound only disabled you, but it could also kill you. If you couldn't get back to the aid station and get proper medical attention within four hours or so, if you didn't get something done for the wound, your whole leg might have to be amputated. The poison went right into the bloodstream. And that was the purpose of it.

The company medic did all he could right there. I called myself hard–core anyway, man. I wouldn't mind going to the rear anytime, I tell you that, but I had partners here. That was the key to the whole deal. You never wanted to be lagging, what we called half–stepping or ghosting. Ghosting was kicking back in the rear. We didn't want to be back there ghosting and have somebody say, "Hey man, your partner got killed." You felt that you could have been there and helped him, you know? That was the kind of understanding we had, man. So I told the medic, "I'm going to try and make it. Try to get that shit out of the wound. Shoot me some morphine and tighten my shit up. I'll be all right." He dug down into it, man. The pungi stick pierced up into the skin and not into the bone. I was lucky on that. He cut the stick out and cleaned the wound out all he could. It was excruciating pain when he started digging in that motherfucker. The morphine helped. I was lucky the wound was near the surface. He kept trying to send me back to the rear. He said, "Man, you better go back. This shit is dangerous." But I kept going for the next couple of days until finally it started to swell.

For the next couple of days we were looking for these guys. We were really pissed because they dusted a couple of our people. We were walking all these miles and my foot was getting sore. Finally it really started to get bad. The jungle boot was rubbing the wound. So they sent me to the rear. I was back there for about a week. I wanted to get back out to the field because I hated the rear.

There wasn't nothing in the rear but a bunch of shit, plus every other night you got mortared. You were like a fucking sitting duck. Maybe Charlie didn't fire much — maybe five or six rounds — but you knew he was there. When he was firing at you, he was trying to say that he was up to something bigger. He wanted you to think that he was attacking you at all times. He might have been thinking to deter you from stopping his main force. If you called Saigon and reported that there was an enemy in the area constantly firing you up, then they'd probably say, "Just pull your men back and protect your perimeter so you don't get overrun." He might only have had a company or even a platoon harassing all around your perimeter. Meanwhile, he was building up for an offensive somewhere else.

So I didn't like the rear area scene. But they had pretty good doctors in the rear. When I went in they cleaned out the wound real good and told me to stay off my feet. I just kicked back till it started to heal. I was there for about a week or so before I went back out to my company.

After I got ready to go back to the company, the doc said, "Maybe you should stay back for another week." "No, I'm ready to hit it." I was bored with the rear. I didn't have no friends back there or nothing. I tried to talk to these guys in the rear, but they were spoons. I never had too much to say to them anyway. Even though they was Americans, it was like they weren't Americans. Plus another thing—we didn't like a lot of them cats for one reason. We believed that they was selling guns and ammo on the black market and that shit was coming back at us out in the bush.

I caught the supply chopper back out to the field. I was glad to get back with the company and they were glad to see me. When I joined up with them they were still chasing the same Vietnamese units up into the mountains toward Dalat.

Stan Goff

Bob Sanders

"It was hot, man."

Busting Bush

Ready for Charlie

Stan and his trumpet

"Smoke bringer"

Sanders, No. 1 machine gunner

Carl and the "pig"

Stan on the road with the M-16

Back in the Boonies

The Long Walk Back

Relaxing at LZ Baldy

Stan at LZ Baldy

Stan shaking hands with General Abrams at conclusion of the
DSC Award Ceremony

THE UNITED STATES OF AMERICA

TO ALL WHO SHALL SEE THESE PRESENTS, GREETING:

THIS IS TO CERTIFY THAT
THE PRESIDENT OF THE UNITED STATES OF AMERICA
AUTHORIZED BY CONGRESS
HAS AWARDED

THE DISTINGUISHED SERVICE CROSS

TO

PRIVATE FIRST CLASS STANLEY C. GOFF, US56835616, UNITED STATES ARMY

FOR

EXTRAORDINARY HEROISM IN ACTION

IN THE REPUBLIC OF VIETNAM ON 25 AUGUST 1968

GIVEN UNDER MY HAND IN THE CITY OF WASHINGTON
THIS   28th   DAY OF FEBRUARY 1969

CREIGHTON W. ABRAMS
General, United States Army
Commanding

SECRETARY OF THE ARMY

The Dead is Going Home

Stan

6 FIRST FIRE FIGHTS

We had been in the boonies for about two months and I'd lost all track of Bob. I'd been carrying the pig for almost six weeks. Now we'd been sent back to Ross. Carl and I went inside of our assigned bunker. "It's not a bad bunker," Carl said. "The only thing about it, man, there's only the two of us. We have to find somebody else to help us pull guard." I said, "No shit, no question about that, man." So he said, "Where's Piper, man?" And I said, "Piper and Baby-san? They gotta be right down there at the other bunker." Earlier the NCO had told us to fill sandbags to reinforce the bunker. He had walked around the bunker and thought the front of it needed more reinforcing. He thought about ten sandbags would do it. I was cleaning my weapon, and I said to Carl, "Well, man, if you fill five, I'll fill five." Carl filled about three and said, "Aw, man, sand-bags . . . that's it. See you later, man. I'm going down to Piper's bunker."

Piper's bunker was only twenty-five yards away. It was about four o'clock in the afternoon. I said, "OK, fine, soon as I finish cleaning my pig, I'll be down." I filled an equal number so there wouldn't be an argument. Then I threw the six sandbags in front of the bunker and left, carrying my pig wrapped around my shoulder, down to Piper's bunker. Apparently the bunker for Piper's squad was OK. When Piper saw me, he said, "Hey, man, how many men do you have over at your bunker?" I said, "We only got two guys." They were all smoking. "Shit, man, there's no use in doing that, man, hell—two guys? And you guys are going to try to pull guard?" "Hey, if we don't get any help, hell no." "Why don't you guys stay up here with us, man, help us all pull guard?" I said, "Yeah, fucking right, make it all easier for you, man, easier for us, no question." Carl said, as he always did, "Yeah, man, right on." Then we all went up to this air strip for some munchies.

I don't know why we felt that we were stealing. The supply sergeant knew damn well who was taking the God damn shit, but he didn't really care. The supply people cared, but only about bringing more boxes down there. So we went up and raided all those boxes of C-rations. We got two or three boxes and stripped all the pound cake and fruit cocktail out. Pound cake and fruit cocktail. Any GI will tell you that it was a delicacy. All GIs can relate to pound cake and fruit cocktail. We had three or four cakes and about three or four cans apiece. We just sat there and munched ourselves into agony.

Later we went back to the bunker and started pulling our guard duty. In the middle of the night we got hit. Rockets. We ran inside of the bunker. Somebody said, "I hope this God damn thing holds." We peered out through the slots to see if we were going to get a ground attack. They had me set up the pig, which they thought was our best defense. The artillery guys had mined outside the whole perimeter, but we didn't hear any mines going off by the barbed wire. Our job was to handle a ground attack in case they tried to rush the compound. It never did materialize. After about twenty minutes of constant barrage, we had an easy night of it, but I was pretty edgy. Hell, I never did go to sleep that night.

Carl and I pulled guard all night at Piper's bunker, with Baby-san, Piper, Belt, and the rest of his crew. The next morning Carl went down to our assigned bunker first, saying, "I'm going to be down there before the CO gets there." I said, "OK, man, that's cool." I was getting my pig ready, then I was on my way down. I saw him standing in front of the bunker shaking his head. I said, "Hey, man, what's wrong?" He pointed and I looked. Apparently during the attack, a VC got close enough to throw a satchel charge. I couldn't tell anything from the front of the bunker. And then I went to the back. I looked down and the whole fucking back of the bunker was blown out. I said, "God damn." He said, "Hey man, if we'd been in there, we'd have been blown to hell." I said, "No shit." We thought how lucky we were that we weren't in that bunker. When we told our platoon sergeant that we had gone down to help Piper pull guard because we didn't have enough men to pull guard ourselves, he didn't do anything except laugh and say, "No problem." But I didn't think it was so funny because we came within a hairline of getting blown to shit.

The rest of our stay at Ross went by pretty uneventful. Later we found out why we were sent back to Ross. They were going to rest us up. They thought that we were seasoned now and they wanted to put us in a major fight. That was what was happening. But I didn't know it then. Nobody knew it. Then we pulled out. At first we were thinking, it had to be something. Then we thought, well, maybe it wasn't. We had a feeling that something wasn't right, that this was too easy, as we got ready to move out on the tenth day.

It was about one o'clock when we gathered down by the gate. We had gotten supplies the day before, anyway. All of a sudden, we saw the CO come down from the colonel's hootch. We knew we was ready to go then. We could read the minds of our officers by their general actions. Our lieutenant went up to him to see exactly what the plan was, and we saw them sort of looking at each other casually, talking and laughing, and we said, "Aw shit, nothing . . ." They were just sort of bullshitting

among each other, cracking jokes. It was a very relaxed atmosphere. When you walked up to your CO, it was a non-officer
approach, you know. The lieutenant was not going to walk up
to the CO and salute him, because Charlie was looking at us,
right there down by the gate. Might have been one of the papa-
sans standing there about to fill sandbags. He might have been
pinpointing who the CO was right there. So it was a very
relaxed thing. He wasn't about to say, "Listen, we're going out
to rendezvous at Hamburger Hill, and this is what we're going
to do," but he might have been giving a code. That was why the
men didn't even know what was happening, because security
might have gotten weakened. The CO would amble around and
mingle with the platoon sergeants. They'd stroll over and
gather around him. They wouldn't rush him. We played the
role. The CO ambled around some more among the men,
maybe about twenty minutes. We hadn't moved. Then some
officers would say, "OK, let's go," just like that and we're gone.

We moved out. We went out the gate and started down
toward the village. Every time we got ready to go out through
the gate, there'd always be about fifty children milling around,
boys and girls from four to fourteen. They probably ended up
being VC. LZ Ross was stationed right above the village. As we
were getting nearer and nearer to this village, we started
gathering a parade. We had all these kids alongside, yelling and
talking. "Hey, GI, hey, GI, you numba one, hey GI . . ." They
were trying to get us to buy things from them like soda pop in
American bottles; but we knew it wasn't American. You could
get ptomaine poisoning. Some guys did drink it sometimes and
survived. Not me. I never bought anything out there, man, not
anything. They were trying to get us to give them something—
"GI, you give me food, you give me food, GI, GI, give me food,
please, please, GI . . ." Some of the guys would throw them
things. By the time we got through the village, there would
probably be a hundred kids. It was a big event for them to see
us go marching down through the village. Everybody'd come
out—the old men, the ladies—everybody yelling and waving,

"GI, GI, you numba one, you numba one." Of course there could have been some VC inside of the houses right then, or *they* could have been VC, themselves. Matter of fact, grenades could have been thrown. We had this on our mind as we walked. Still we couldn't help but get enthused with all the excitement generated around us. It wasn't like we were going to a fire fight. This was nothing but a working day for us. We were just enjoying it because we were leaving the base. We were thinking to ourselves, "Jesus, I wish I had nothing to do but sit out here and watch GIs going down the street. I wish I had nothing else to do except come down here and kick back and relax, and have mama-san cook me some rice and meat." We really weren't thinking about where we were going. A grunt didn't care where he was going. We weren't going to find out anyway, except when we knew we were going to see some heavy activity. Obviously we wanted to be warned if we were going to see some shit. And we always were. But at this particular point, we had not yet been warned about anything like that. As we got further and further out, the kids started dropping off. Soon they'd be all gone. We were still mainly talking, bullshitting. As we got about three hours out from the base, orders came down to cut the bullshit.

We began to wonder where the hell we were going now. Pretty soon we were walking on a dirt road, white sand, hard top. I didn't believe it'd be too hard when the rains came, but at that moment it was. As we walked along we saw all these remnants of mansions that had been blown apart during the French war, and obviously, from the heavy attacks by B-52s, too. We saw patches and patches of rice paddies. Nobody was working the rice paddies, nobody. I thought, all this land, going to waste. There probably would have been thousands and thousands of people working those rice paddies at one time. They were really huge; as big as a lake, as far as the eye could see.

We didn't see any people at all as we got further and further out. The people back in that village were all surviving off LZ

Ross, living under our protection. If the village got any heavy activity, LZ Ross would have sent a company down there just like that. The LZ lived off the village too. A lot of men lived on an LZ—from six to nine hundred, maybe a thousand men, depending on its size. So you had to figure, the base could have lasted a long time with the LZ protecting the village, and the village serving the LZ's needs and desires, and the black market flourishing.

We continued walking and finally got off this road. It was getting narrower and narrower, slowly turning into a trail. As we got off, we moved through the bush in single file. That night we noticed we were on white sand. We were near the beach, by the China Sea. I didn't know it at the time. Nobody else did. We pulled into a fairly flat area with small sagebrush–like bushes, about two to three feet high. I didn't see any trees at all, just these little sage bushes everywhere, and I said, "Jesus Christ, if we get hit, there's no place really to hide." And everybody said, "No God damn lie." "We might be hit," and we all said, "Aw, fuck." Nobody wanted to dig in. So we were all moaning and groaning about whether we were going to dig in; the ground seemed pretty stable, but that was debatable too. Everybody started debating on whether, when we were getting a mortar attack, it'd be better to be in a hole or on a flat open surface. Finally the word got around from the CO that there was no problem; we didn't have to dig in. So we started setting up.

By that time the company was seasoned; we'd been together a long time now. I had been in the boonies myself for about three months, so I was getting to be a pro. After sixty days in the boonies, you should know what the hell you're doing. By ninety days, you were finished being a rookie. I was squad leader by now. So I was setting up the pig; my squad—me and Carl— were spreading out. We were expecting to get two new men. When you set up, you tried to find your best possible defensive way to stop Charlie. You tried to find the weakest area in your linkage with the rest of the company. You set up an area where you thought Charlie might think he had an advantage and try to creep in. Carl and I decided to set up right on top of a hill with an easy slope downward. Charlie could easily have got down in this area, and sneaked up on us. We wanted to set right on top of the hill, rather than set back from the slope. That way I could see down in the slope. Then we put the five claymore mines at the bottom of the slope, so that if he approached the slope, they could blow him away. It was up to the platoon sergeant to make sure that the men had secure positions. The entire company perimeter was set up in a wagon train circle. The wider the circle, the better. You didn't want to get it too small, in case of grenades or mortars, or hand–to–hand combat. That evening, after we set up, we heard the helicopter come in. Guys shouted, "Hey, Huey landing," and word got around that a helicopter was bringing men and supplies, and mail — that was exciting.

The company got two brand new men. So we said, "Oh, got a couple of greenhorns here. Shit, man, wonder whose squad are they going to? We need them." And sure enough, they came to our squad. One guy's name was Emory. He was a guy that ended up getting a Silver Star. He was the guy that went with me when we got to the big battle. He was from Oklahoma. Both were white guys, but I can't remember the other guy's name, just a quiet guy. Did his work, obeyed his orders and sort of talked with Emory all the time. Another guy had transferred over so that meant I had four men in my squad. It was finally complete, a five–man squad. Right away, I started orienting the new guys about what to do, the same way they oriented me when I got into the field: "OK, now listen — where you from, man?" "Oh, I'm from Oklahoma." "Is that right? Long way from home." "Yeah." I said, "All right, now listen, this is Carl." "What's happening?" "Oh, not too much, man, not too much." "This is JJ." "What's going on?" "Not too much . . . ."

Nothing really happened the next three days. The guys placed the claymore mines out just exactly as I told them. They all carried their ammo. In my squad I must have had about three thousand rounds. I was wondering why we got so much ammunition. Usually I carried about eighteen hundred rounds. I thought, Jesus, we had a lot of ammo. Maybe we're going to be out longer than I thought we were . . . . Then all of a sudden, we were told that we were going to walk back in a different direction. We hadn't seen the ocean yet and were moving back from it. The guys were complaining, "We didn't even see the ocean, man, where we going? We're moving out of here?" Everybody was moaning and groaning. The CO and the NCOs were just bullshitting with them, and telling them nothing: "You'll see it next time. Shut the hell up." So we started moving out and all of a sudden, I'll be damned if we didn't see . . . . "Hey, man, army personnel carriers. Hey, there's a cavalry unit up here, man. Hey, man, we're approaching a cavalry unit." "A cavalry unit?" "Yeah, man." "What the hell's going now?" We're all perked up, looking and straining, and sure enough, they were pushing up all kinds of heavy artillery — "God damn, what's happening?"

Walking up, we saw army personnel carriers, armed with 50–caliber machine guns; we saw tanks up there, and we said, "Wow." It was the first time I'd seen tanks out in the field myself, so I was pretty excited. Everybody else was, too. All these tank units really looked fearsome. They were just sitting in a big wide semicircle, the engines not running, which was why we didn't hear them. They told us they were the 86th Mechanized Cavalry, part of the 1st Cavalry Division, yellow patch with a black horse on it. All together there were probably thirty units — tanks and APCs. We just walked right into the semicircle. When I saw those tanks, it made me feel this was really a war! And they looked as though they had gone through some shit. They were working tanks, not brand new and sparkling. The personnel carriers were all dusty, with ragged, tattered sandbags all over them, looking like they'd been in action.

At first, I hadn't thought about the seriousness of meeting with this Cav unit. You know how naive I am. I just thought we gonna ride for a while. Almost immediately, we were told to mount up on the carriers. My squad got up on one of the APCs. They were waiting for us; that was why they were there —a rendezvous. We didn't know it; we never knew anything. As we mounted up and started moving out, we talked to the guys in the APC. "Hey, man, where we going, man?" They said, "Shit, man, we don't know. We were just told to meet you out here." So we were all bullshitting with these guys. "Hey, man, how's it feel to ride?" "Shit, I'd rather be walking. We can get blown out of here. This is nothing but a God damn cracker box." And it was true. They were vulnerable, because once the NVA penetrated their defensive line, and there were so many of them where they couldn't successfully be kept off, and if the APC driver and gunners were not good, it was like being in a cracker box. Once the NVA got through and dropped even one grenade, that thing would be blown to shit.

All of a sudden I started figuring, well, God damn, we had to be going to some shit. It just struck me out of a clear blue sky. My mind started moving again. I said, "Man, we gotta be doing something. They don't take us out of nowhere by cavalry unit to an R & R." It turned out that we went all the way back out to where we had been. They carried us back onto the damn beach. We went right out to the sea, and we were all yelling, "Hey, man, there's the sea, man, isn't that beautiful—hey, man, let's go surfing, man? Are you taking this God damn thing in the water, man?" All the units pulled up on the beach in a sort of parallel assault line and we all got off.

Nobody knew what to do at first. We just hung around near the APC. I told my squad, "Hold up, man, don't go walking around yet. You don't know what's happening now." So Carl said, "Aw, God damn, there's Daddy Goff . . . ." I said, "Oh shut up, Carl, God damn it, you know we don't know what's happening, man. Shut the fuck up, willya." Finally the NCO walked by and said, "We're gonna be here for a spell, Goff, so just rest your men." "All right—you guys heard it." The driver of the APC told me there was a large NVA regiment around. "We've been following them for weeks. When we get in the thick underbrush we're stuck." "OK, I see. But they're not out here at the beach. Shit, we've got to go back about thirty clicks." That was why they had picked us up. If we had to walk thirty clicks, it would have taken us weeks. We were told that we could swim if we wanted to. So we all stripped down and went out there in the beautiful China Sea and swam for an hour in squads. As far as the eye could see, nothing but beautiful blue water and white sand. There was no surf whatsoever, just sort of ripples. The water seemed about ninety degrees. I will never forget that beach as long as I live.

That night was uneventful and the next morning we moved out of that area. We traveled with those personnel carriers all day long, going inland. We started getting into trees and heavy brush. Matter of fact, I had to soften my seat, because riding on the damn thing was getting so hard. But, hell, I really enjoyed the ride. That night we set up. Setting up guard with the guys from carriers was a breeze, really nice to do. Since they all helped pull guard, which was only about thirty minutes, we ended up sleeping seven hours or so, and that was really great.

The next day, we were put on alert. We were told not to sit lazily on the carriers but expect to jump off. We were given orders before we moved out what to do if the carrier got hit. We continued to ride, looking for this NVA regiment. Finally, after the third day, it was like we'd been on the carriers ever since I'd been in-country. Soon, a whole week went by. We felt pretty good. Only thing about it, we knew eventually we were going to meet some shit.

At this point, I had to switch over and ride on a tank for a while. It was really something riding on a tank. Those things just rolled over things. They were just going up and down. It was like the whole thing was so big, when it went up, you were going up towards the sky, like riding on a mountain. These guys didn't stop for ten-foot high trees; hey, right over the top. Gone. Just gone. Those things were gruesome.

After about a week, we were getting into country where we knew we were going to get into activity. Word got around that we knew where the NVA were, but we were ready. We were told to clean our weapons, make sure we were ready to go, to expect contact anytime. So everybody was pretty sober that day. Nobody was bullshitting. We weren't told how many or what, but we knew we were looking for a big NVA regiment that had a reputation. We'd heard that they had met the Marines up in Dak To and just kicked the shit out of them. I was anticipating my major event of the war.

Stan

7 THE BIG BATTLE

That day, as I remember, we started going real, real slow. We were riding along in a thick woody area, and all of a sudden, out of a clear blue sky, we heard a "boom bam . . . DIDIDI DIDI . . ." The APC stopped and we jumped off and got down beside the tanks. We were looking, trying to figure what was happening. It was way in the back. When you had thirty-five mechanized vehicles, you had to figure this entourage was a huge thing—like a wagon train, it was so damn long. Of course, they knew we were coming. What happened was that one of the carriers got hit. It wasn't a bad hit, but the five guys on top of it got blasted by a shell that hit the side of the carrier. So we had to stop and wait; my squad just stayed put. We didn't know whether we were going to get hit with another rush or not. We just stayed behind the thing. We sat there and waited until the medivac came in and carried the five guys away.

Slowly we found out what happened. One guy got his arm almost torn off; another guy got hit in the eye. Damn! So we said, "Well, this is the shit. This is what we've been riding so

God damn long for." We were moving toward the major conflict. By this time, we were all ready for it. "Let's get it on.
Fucking bastards." We were cussing them out, all of us, because
it was mostly brothers that got it that day, guys we knew.
"Eugene got it man?" "Yeah, man, he got half his fucking arm
torn off." "Anyway, he's going home?" "Yeah." "He got outa
here . . ." Throughout the war, no matter how you got out, even
if you got a leg blown off you, you got out alive. Your time
was up. But it was *the way* you got out that was the significance. That was what the American people didn't realize, how
tough it was. To be hit and have his arm torn off, that was like
somebody giving him two hundred thousand dollars. That was
how much his life was worth. His arm. To get out of the war,
his contract was his arm.

I guess the caravan stopped about an hour. Then we started
moving again. We knew we had to get the assault in the backs
of our minds, because the next tank to get his could be us. So
we rode along and I thought about what we were going to do
if we got hit. If they came out of the bushes right now, what
was I going to do? I had the pig in a ready position and I was
going to sling it right down and start spraying. That was all I
was thinking. The carriers were lined up at the edge of this one
huge rice paddy. They started coming alongside each other,
but we weren't told to dismount. So we still stayed on them while
they were getting into position. Nobody told us that anything
was over across the paddy at all. Nobody said, "OK, there's
an NVA regiment over there. Go get 'em." All we knew was
that there was a woodline over there.

I never will forget how we approached it, the tanks and
APCs quietly lining up in parallel formation. The rice paddy
was about two times the length of a football field and about a
football field in width. I heard guys mumbling, but I was just
listening for a command, which could come from anyone, like
the driver. Everything was moving so fast. Within a fifteen-
minute interval we stopped and lined up at the rice paddy.
Then the word came, "All right, dismount and stay at the back

of the carriers." So the men started to climb down the sides of the vehicles. All of a sudden, the carriers started reconning by fire. They just started firing at this woodline, "Boom, boom," with all these big tank guns, just tearing that fucking woodline all up. Man, the whole damn woodline opened up, "BOOM didididid wham WHAM . . ." Rockets. I heard guys getting hit from over to my left. I heard a tank get hit. I didn't know how bad.

Now my mind was jumping. By this time everybody was reconning by fire. I was firing back automatically even while this barrage was coming in. Everybody was standing up there doing nothing but firing like hell. Pretty soon we were told, "Back up, back up, back up, we're going to be backing up, pull back." So we started pulling back. I thought to myself, "God damn. Shit. Fuck it, it's hell over there . . ." This regiment probably had left a suicide battalion over there to knock shit out of us, so that the rest of the enemy could go on and do what they had to do. We pulled back into the opposite woodline.

While I pulled myself together, I was looking around for my men. They were really shaken up. I could see the shock in their faces—no blood at all in their faces. They said, "Hey, man, are we gonna go across to that woodline?" I said, "Yup, I think we are." "Oh, man, that's suicide." "Could possibly be, man." I didn't know what was going on toward the other end of the column. There was our whole fucking company here, 125 men; add the cav unit, and there were three hundred men, easily. Our company was beefed up and now I knew why. After we pulled back into the woodline, I made sure that my weapon was clean. That was what my squad saw me doing.

I never will forget Piper looking at me and shaking his head. It looked as if he was almost ready to cry, because he knew we might be looking at each other for the last time. And I guess there was a sort of unity between Piper and me, because politically he had tried to make every man see the full thing of what our country was doing. Here it was, just taking us to our death. We were nothing but bodies, that was all; out for a huge body count. And this was it; just setting us up for this race across that paddy. I saw the hurt in his face as he looked at me. Because I had the pig, I guess he thought his brother might get blown away. I took my eyes away from him, because I said to myself, "I'm not going to think about that, I don't want to think about that. I'm not going to get blown away." But I knew the look —he looked at me as though I was a dead man. I guess he figured he would stand a chance of surviving—but the pig— everybody was going to shoot at the pig.

Soon we heard a helicopter come in. They were medivacking guys. One of the tanks was blown away; it took a direct hit. I think we lost that tank and a carrier in the fighting, so they evacuated that team. Somebody asked, "When are they going to send in the planes?" A lot of guys thought they were going to send in planes.

And then we found out that we were actually going to assault that woodline. "Assault on the woodline?" a lot of guys were saying. I wasn't saying anything. "Oh, man, these mother-fuckers—"guys were bitching. Then all of a sudden we heard the CO say, "SHUT UP, and that's an order! I mean it, God damn it. Now, we're going to assault this fucking woodline and that's that." An order. Other than the original recon by fire, there was no artillery on the woodline. The CO said the next man that opened his God damn mouth would be court-martialed. We got ready to assault the woodline.

I got my weapon all cleaned and made sure that all my guys were around me, and I didn't do too much talking. I said, "OK, men. Primarily what I want you to do is just stick by me, OK? Emory, when I call for that ammo, I want you to have your ass right here—you got it?" "I got it, Goff, OK." "OK, fine, just keep your head down, man." "OK." And I thought to myself, "This little fucker sure has a lot of balls." I mean, never once, all the time he'd been in–country did I ever see him blink. I sort of favored him over the rest of the guys, even Carl, because I knew what Carl would do. Emory would never have any type of fear or apprehension. I never did even see him swallow hard. He'd only been in–country about six, eight weeks. Here he was, about to see the biggest battle of his whole life—and he was just sitting there, drinking in every word I told him. He stared me right in the eyes, as I stared him right back, and he just drank in every word I told him. I don't know, I guess some of the other guys thought that I was gung ho, and, to a certain degree, they were trying to stay away from me. But he didn't. And then again, Carl, and the other three guys knew that I was vulnerable with the pig, too. When I found out that Emory wasn't gun-shy like that, wasn't so paranoid, I really took to him. He had most of my ammo.

You see, a gunner needed an ammo bearer that was not so worried about his own head that he couldn't effectively feed the gunner the ammo. I would be blowing lead out of that pig so quick I'd go through a belt in ten seconds, needed a man to be able to hand me the ammo. He didn't have to stick it in the weapon. I did that. He just simply handed it to me, and I flopped it in there. I could do it faster than he could, anyway.

As we got ready to go back up to the woodline, the NVA stopped firing, waiting for us to charge. It was very quiet over there. Then the tanks moved out and started firing as they went, the NVA returning their fire. We all started moving out too, walking at first, just walking behind the tanks, letting them do all the firing. As the fire came in, I heard it hit on the top of the tank that I was behind—ding, dang, ding. As the tanks started going faster and faster, they cut us loose as they got ahead of us. Obviously, as that cover pulled out about ten feet ahead, we started lowering ourselves and we started firing. As they finally pulled away from us, we all hit the dirt, out in the middle of the rice paddy, and started inching our way toward the dike. Then we were all running toward the first dike with the tanks forty feet ahead. We couldn't fire too much because they were still too close to us. So we mostly kept our heads down and moved toward that first dike, about two feet high—high enough for protection. As infantry, our job was to take care of the NVA who might have moved on foot to attack the tanks and the personnel carriers from the rear.

As the tanks moved forward, they were shooting like hell,

burning up the people in the woodline. My squad was to my immediate right. We were getting all kinds of pig firepower from that brush and all the way to the left. I couldn't see what was happening at the other end of the company; I only knew what was going on in the 2nd platoon.

Now, what were they going to do? The NVA were sitting back there and waiting for us to actually try and attack them head on. What were we going to do? The NVA's sole intent was to have us try to attack them, and they were going to circle us and cut us off from the rear. That was the whole trip.

I was at the dike, firing like hell with Emory right with me, just handing me that lead. He said, "Hey, Goff, I'm out of lead. What do you want to do?" "Don't worry, I got enough right down here," and I was still firing. "What I want you to do is go and get all the ammo from the other guys down at the other end of the company. Find anybody that's got ammo, just get it."

So this kid, on his hands and knees, crawled along in back of the dike, collecting ammo and bringing it back up to me, and I was firing like hell. I probably went through two thousand rounds. Everybody was depending on Goff right then; Goff was the firepower. And I knew I was quieting that area, because my firepower was very effective. As I was running I was steadily blowing out lead. I saw these guys moving around in the woodline. But primarily I wasn't looking at the guys; I was only looking at the angling of my weapon and where my firepower was going. That was the only thing I was worrying about. And as I was going, I was steadily laying down my firepower so effectively that I was just not getting hit myself. That's the only explanation I can come up with.

Emory and I were running up and down this rice paddy firing. The guys would tell me, "Hey, Goff, right here, right in there, man." I would sit down between two guys and blow out where they thought they were getting heavy concentration of fire. Then Emory and I would run into another area along the dike. When Sergeant Needham hollered, "Goff, Goff, over here man, I got thirty or forty of them, right there, right there," I'd fire

right where he told me to fire. Those were the thirty or forty
NVA I am accredited with in that area. Emory was not with
me. I told him to stay while I ran over and was firing my ass
off in this particular area, so he started firing his M–16, too.

We were in the middle of the paddy at the first dike, which
we went over. We cut down that body of men so well, knocked
out their firepower, that we could move now on toward the
second dike at the end of the paddy, firing steadily. After we
got to the second dike, I went on firing for about fifteen more
minutes, but then my pig fell apart. It just blew up in the
air like it did earlier at the creek. This time the barrel did
fine, but the pins came out of the side of the weapon. It just
got too hot, and when it expanded, the pins and the locks and
the keys that held it in place were no longer workable, and the
pig just came apart. It came apart in my hands. The top of the
tray popped up; it was sprung, and I couldn't keep it down. I
couldn't fire without the tray being down. By that time there
was hardly any activity. I was still staring at the woodline, and
the guys saw how it was. "Goff, are you all right?" Emory
said, "Are you all right, man?" "Yeah, I'm fine, man." Just
exhausted as hell, I could hardly talk, my whole mouth was
so dry. I was slumped on my knees at the second dike, just
staring. The second dike was almost at the woodline. With us
being at the woodline and me sitting there exhausted, and with
the area completely quieted, a few of the other squads started
to run into the woodline, crouched, searching, looking,
weapons at the ready.

They started taking a body count. That was when the CO
went into the woodline — to see if they could find any prisoners
or whatever. But I'd done most of the work. The rest of the guys
were sitting. I'd been doing all the running, so I was dead to
the world. The guys just told me to sit there, because my pig
was out of action. They got me Juju's pig; he was the other
gunner. They told me to sit there while they went to take a body
count, which they did. I just sat there with my men and held
down the rest of the platoon.

So after that, the main body of men were told to pull out of the dike area and move on up to the grounds of this plantation. We were still firing, taking in rounds over on our right as we moved up. It was coming out of the woods on the right flank. I never will forget this area. Did you ever see grading crews on the road? That's how the whole area looked, obviously from the tanks that went into this area. I was on my knees sweating profusely.

Then we started moving toward another dike about two or three feet high. As I went, I sort of lost my head; I mean I wasn't thinking too clearly. My helmet had fallen off and I knew it was off, but I didn't try to stop and get it even though rounds were still coming in. I didn't see anything in front of me, but I heard the tanks yards and yards ahead of us, way down on the right flank. We were told to wait at the little wall, that the tanks were going to come back for us. Three tanks came back for us. During the battle they were way in front of us. They had gone into the woods only so far and decided to come back and pick up the company. We assumed that our orders were to move after the retreating NVA. That was why they came back and picked us up. We'd blown away their line, so we were going in after them.

I was groggy, but we had to move out; so what if I was groggy! I could hardly get up on top of the God damn tank, I was so weak. Sitting up there, I saw all these bodies, or parts of bodies—hands, arms—so much so that it was making me sick to see all these bodies lying on the ground. I realized that it could have been me down there. That was what I kept thinking. I'd just look off into the woods and see rows of bodies, NVA soldiers with backpacks on, T-shirts, parts of uniforms. Obviously, the NVA had tried to strip the bodies as much as they possibly could, to try to prevent us from knowing what rank they were. They'd take anything of value. There were all kinds of dirt marks dug into the ground. From where my tank was it was hard to tell the tank gashings in the dirt from streaks where bodies had been dragged away. But you knew they had dragged away as many bodies as they could. There were blood marks in the dirt. I got tired of looking. I thought to myself, "See, that's what we were doing."

We moved on the pursuit then. We drove about twenty minutes, traveled about a click down into this deep gulley. Then the orders changed. I don't know why. We turned around and came back to the plantation house on the outskirts of the original rice paddy. We dismounted and I walked about ten or fifteen feet up to the porch and collapsed. "I can't move." It was no laughing matter then. I was conked out on the ground. And I stayed there. My sense at that time was that I had just been in a helluva battle, and that I had done nothing more than anybody else did; that I had done nothing outstanding, but that I was alive; I had survived. I hadn't even gotten hit. And at the same time, I was wondering how many people were hit, how many men had we lost? I was laying down there on this ground, and I was looking up at the sky. Finally I just closed my eyes and thought, man, if somebody came along right now and shot the shit out of me, he'd just have to do it, cause aside from the fact I was breathing, I was dead anyway. I just had to lay there, just try to get myself rejuvenated. I was completely wasted. I was shaking, just out of it.

Then I heard the medic walk up. Doc took a look at me, said, "Goff, are you all right?" I said, "Yeah, yeah, I'm all right. I'm all right, Doc, just tired." "Yeah, we all are." He walked away. Then I heard the sergeant and the CO come up. I thought I heard them say something like, "This guy did a hell of a job." I thought to myself, "CO says I did a hell of a job." It made me feel good, like any compliment to somebody for working hard. At that particular time I didn't care, except that I did a good job according to the company commander. That the company commander would notice you, out of a hundred men, that would make you feel good. So after that, the medivacs were coming in and carrying guys that had been hit out of the field. I heard pros like Piper saying, "Oh, man, another fucking Khe Sanh." I knew that I had survived a major battle.

Stan

8 SEARCH AND DESTROY

They asked me did I want to go in? "No, man, I don't want to go in." I knew that to go to the LZ for one fucking day and then come back out was nothing. I mean, what the hell? I thought, get on that helicopter, get blown away, fuck it, I was alive right now and I was on this ground, let's keep it that way. So I said, "Hell no, I'm all right." After that, they flew in hot chow, the whole God damn thing. Something like that, they were going to fly in some hot chow. We were told the Cav unit guys got hot food flown in every day. I finally got up after about an hour and walked around shakily, finding my strength returning. After I walked some, the blood started circulating in my body, so I went down into a big hollowed-out gulley, like a deep encavement. By now the tanks had all re-formed and were in a big perimeter around us, making us feel fairly safe from an assault, which could occur at any time. Down in this gulley I saw guys getting ready to fly out; bandages all over their arms, legs, what have you. But they weren't from my platoon.

Then they brought in the jets and we got ready to pull out.

This was the first time I'd seen Phantoms. They pulled an air strike in that mountainous area where the NVA had retreated. While they did that our unit pulled out. It was late in the afternoon. We went back across that rice paddy, and as I walked I thought, God damn, this motherfucker here got a whole lot of guys fucked up. And it could have been the end of my road, right there. In my company, we lost five guys, but no one from my platoon.

On our way, we watched the demolition team blow apart a tank that had been hit. We didn't want Charlie to get anything off it he could use. Back in the wooded area we started moving into different terrain. We thought at first we were going back the way we came but found out later that we weren't. Moving along the woodline, I had my weapon at the ready, but for some reason I didn't think about getting hit. I don't know why. Maybe that was the way GIs had to think—if we got hit, fine; if we didn't, fine. The reality was that we were not in control, so why be all nervous about it? You didn't have any special emotions about dying. I especially didn't after I saw those bodies just laying down there. They looked sort of plastic-like. As it got to be dusk, we set up for that night in a quiet, wooded area. We had seven guys to pull guard duty, so it was really a breeze.

The next day, as we approached a wide-open area, we realized we were to rendezvous with a much larger troop unit. We saw about a hundred men spread out, and we said, "Damn, that means that we're going to be getting into some other heavy fight." What happened was that the battalion headquarters was still looking for the remainder of that NVA regiment we were originally after. So they rendezvoused us with another hundred men already in this area. We dismounted and started bull-shitting with them. They had already heard about the shit that we'd been in. They saw us: "Hey, man?" We saw a few guys that were green. We knew they were green cause their uniforms weren't old at all. "Hey, man, what about that shit you guys just got out of?" "Yeah, man, it was a real heavy, man. We ran into a thousand guys up there." "That right, man?" "Yeah, man." "NVA?" "Yeah, NVA." "God damn. I understand that's what we got up here, man." "What's happening up here?" I said, "This must be that NVA regiment we're looking for." "Yeah, that's what it is."

All of a sudden we started to line up for an on line assault, with a parallel line of tanks and armored personnel carriers with twin 50-caliber machine guns in front of us. To my right and left, the assault line was as far as the eye could see in both directions. It was about two o'clock in the afternoon. We went through the same procedure that we did once before. First, all the guys reconned by fire, firing like hell. Then we got twice our fire back. I thought to myself, "Seems like I've heard this before." I was joking now, but, "God damn, here we go again." I got my ammo all up, Emory right beside me. We looked at each other and smiled. As we started moving out across this wide open area toward a woodline, the fire got more intense. A tank got hit (almost identical situation) and we pulled back.

Apparently the other company kept going up into the woods. They had some ego-type CO — see, the whole war was actually ego. That company just got there, right? And we already had a big body count; so they had to get a body count. He carried his company on up into the woods to try to flank the NVA. We were pulling back to try to medivac these tank guys that had been hit. Another guy almost got run over by an APC. It was very dangerous when these big carriers were in front of you maneuvering around, skidding around like hell, showering lead this way and that way. If you got caught in the middle of that, that was just all over for you, brother. I can't tell you how fast, how alert we had to be out there. We were all eighteen, nineteen, twenty — all young and fast. We were jumping out of the way of these vehicles and still we had to fire all the damn time. It was a hell of a trip out there.

We found out through the shouting of the gunners on the tracks that Charlie was dug in, in bunkers up there. In the meantime, this other company had got its ass going up through that woodline, still firing. We got the order to pull back out of firing range. We sat behind a column of tanks behind this rice paddy dike and began to think. Dug in bunkers. Now this is some different shit. I hoped we didn't have to try rushing any fucking bunkers. They had automatic weapons inside of them. I was sitting down with Emory looking at me. He said, "Automatic weapons? Bunkers, man?" I said, "Yeah, listen—when we rush a bunker, man, fuck trying to fire, you keep your ass down on the ground, you understand? Our main thing is, to try to get as close as possible."

What the hell would you want to try to fire at a bunker for? It was a waste of time. What you tried to do was fake him off, get close, and then fire the hell at him so he'd keep his head tucked inside that damn bunker until you could get around him and could toss something inside. But that was heavy, man, very hard to do, specially if you had a crack shot inside there behind that automatic weapon. He had a machine gun, too.

Then, all of a sudden, I heard that we were going to have a jet strike. And man, when I heard those jets overhead, I grinned at Emory. I said, "Oh, wow—outstanding!" The tanks were in front of me. I heard the jets. These things were happening in split second sequences, and we were pulling back. A helicopter was coming in. Somebody was hit, the medivac was on the horn, calling. All these things were happening at once. The other company was way up inside the woodline, firing like hell up there. We were pulling back and my squad was looking at each other, just waiting. What was the main body of us going to do? I didn't know what the next order was going to be.

When the jets came, the other company began trying to pull their men out. But they left fifteen bodies up there, men who were walking point in their company. Nobody was going to do anything until they'd pulled that strike, but the jets had to wait till the company pulled out. All this was supposed to take about ten or fifteen minutes.

The strike must have lasted about thirty minutes. The jets came in pouring napalm. They dropped napalm canisters on the trees. I saw dozens of trees disintegrate before my eyes; the limbs came right out. About three hundred of us saw that. "Oh, now let's see, that's probably about a hundred thousand dollars over there." "Yeah, I'd say that was worth, what do you say man? About seventy-five thousand?" "Oh, that's probably about 150 grand." You know, the cost of the bombs they dropped. We were all kidding, joking as they were dropping. We were mystified, too, at seeing the power of the destruction, the audacity of us being able to drop this kind of destructive materials. I was thinking to myself, "Incredible. How can a man *order* something like that on somebody?" When they dropped napalm, it sheered an area the size of a football field. I saw on this whole mountainside nothing left except a black area. They dropped on these bunkers and it was quiet after that, probably burned all those guys up inside. We didn't go up to find out what kind of damage we did; not to that area. But there were fifteen bodies to the right of us in a heavy wooded area.

I don't know why our company ended up having to go in there. The other company lost the men. But I understood half that company was green, anyway. I don't know what the logic was, but we had to go up there and get them. Maybe I'm wrong. Maybe Captain Milpas, when he reads this, will say, "No, Goff, those men were in your company." I know that those fifteen men were not in my platoon; maybe it was in my own company, which was why we got involved. Anyway, after the strike was over, they sent my platoon in. I don't know how many other platoons, but I know we started heading up into that woodline, single file, keeping our heads down. At the same time, the tanks pulled back. They were going to lay fire up over our heads in the wooded area where there might be snipers. As they were firing through the treetops, they were just shearing branches, and the branches were falling on us while the lead was sizzling overhead. We kept our heads down. As we got up nearer, we started hearing AK-47s. There's always a difference. You could always tell that weapon, boy, really a weird, shrill type of sound. You knew it like the back of your hand. The entire forest filled up with smoke, noise, branches falling. That was when one of the men in my squad freaked out.

The platoon leader called for the pig. When my man heard the order, his nerve snapped. He said, "The hell with it, Goff, I'm not going any more. I'm not going any more." I said, "What the hell are you talking about, you not going any more?" "You hear me. I'm not going up there to get killed." I said, "Look, God damn it, you move your ass up. You get your ass off that fucking ground and let's go. The order says to move up. We are going on up to get those bodies and that's it." "God damn it, I'm not going . . ." "You sorry motherfucker, I should blow your God damn brains away." "Well, go ahead and do it, just go ahead and do it. I'm not moving." So I just looked at the guy.

I basically understood his logic. It seemed like genocide— all us blacks out there in the boonies. We'd all talked about this. He was black. I thought fuck it, let this guy alone. Let him go home to his mama. Hell. To a certain degree, deep down inside, I didn't blame him. I didn't blame him one fucking bit. What I said was, "You better be glad it's me, though, and nobody else." I was taking another risk, because, in the meantime, I'd send my men on up while I stayed to convince him to go. I was taking the chance that this fellow could blow my head off as I walked away from him. I was the only guy that knew he sat there and disobeyed an order. This man could have been court-martialed, sent to Leavenworth for fifteen years.

He said, "I know how I look, man. I'm a coward. You can call me any God damn thing you want. You can tell the CO. I'm not going up there." He just lost all of his nerve; he couldn't take it. So I walked away from him.

My squad had gone up to where the battle was real thick. We were getting incoming resistance from Charlie, up inside this thick woodline. We couldn't go any further. The trail was falling off into an area very thick with vines. My squad was on its hands and knees. Then the platoon lieutenant said, "Goff, I need some volunteers. I need five volunteers to go up with me to get those bodies." I said, "You got it." I was getting ready to go up with him, and then he said, "No, fuck it. Tell you what, Goff, let me have the pig. I want you to go back down and get litters and bring them up."

The CO and the first lieutenant apparently found out from the radio that a guy was wounded up there. There was another squad up there. Three or four guys were pinned down right in front of them. They were in a fire fight and Charlie was trying to keep them from getting the bodies. We were trying to get those bodies and the wounded guys out. They had their legs all squashed and smashed in, so they couldn't move. That was why they needed a litter. So he sent me back down to the edge of the woodline. He said, "You can't take anybody with you, Goff. I want you to go down there and go fast." I said, "Ok, fine." He said, "Here, take the M-79."

I took an M-79 and started running double time, triple time, really. I ran back down through the brush, by where this guy had refused to move. He was still down on all fours, and as he saw me go by him, he said, "Goff." He looked at me and I looked back at him. I was going to blow him away if he tried to aim a weapon at me, because I thought maybe he'd try to kill me. He said, "Goff," and I looked at him. "You're a damn fool." I said, "Yeah, you're right," and I turned. I kept going. I don't know why. I felt as if he was going to blow me away, he'd just have to do it. I didn't have time to deal with him. I felt in my own mind that those guys that lay up there wounded were more important. And me getting that litter back up there. I zigzagged myself around so fast that if he tried to take a shot at me, he couldn't have hit me. I went all the way back down to where the tanks were and got the litters, but as I was turning around and getting ready to go back, my platoon sergeant said, "Goff, that's enough." I said, "What do you mean, that's enough?" "You're not to go up there. That's all right. You stay here." So he didn't let me go back up there. A tank went up as far as it could go, and the guys that were on the tank took the litters on up, I guess. I didn't see it. I just saw the tank moving out.

By this time, I noticed that guys were looking at me sort of strange. You know what I mean? You could feel it: "That's the guy, right there." That type of look coming from them. It was a look of, "This guy's looking after more than himself, and he's going to get his fucking ass blown away." Earlier, the platoon sergeant gave me a big long speech about not trying to be a hero. Things go to a person's head. People that have in a single instant displayed extraordinary ability, really start thinking that they are superhuman. And they probably get blown away too. It's nothing other than faith. Faith makes people do extraordinary things. That's a known phenomenon. The platoon sergeant didn't want me to start psyching my mind to the point where I thought I couldn't get killed. He knew that I volunteered to get the wounded and was sent back down through the woodline to get the litters. That was enough, I guess he thought, that guy needed a rest. I was near the point where I was expendable to myself. Anyway, this platoon sergeant ordered me not to go back to my squad. I watched the tank going up there and I knew they got the bodies and the wounded out. So it was a successful rescue mission.

That night we pulled guard in that same area, and the next morning we pulled out. We didn't go back to LZ Ross. We kept moving, on a Search and Destroy. We knew that they was just keeping us moving, but resting us up. We knew that they had taken us out of a heavy fighting zone and put us in a light contact zone. Maybe the general liked us.

About three days after the battle, my squad went out reconning. We must have gone out about a mile from the company — just our own little Search and Destroy mission. We got out as far as we wanted to go and then set up. I used to get my guard up by having each guy facing in another direction. We just sat there bullshitting, but I made sure they had their weapons at the ready. I always kept them on edge. They knew that. That was why they always called me Daddy Goff. My orders would be, "Your weapon cleaned?" "Yeah." "Got your ammo?" "Yep." "OK, you can freak out now." Just as long as I knew they had their shit in order, in case we got hit. That day was such a dull day that I started to tear down my pig. For me to tear down my pig, they knew, I must have been convinced there was nothing out there. I had the radio with me, and all of a sudden we got word to come in. But first I heard the activity—AK-47, "dididididi shoom shoom . . . "—and I heard some guys yelling in the distance. We were less than a mile away. One guy shouting sounded like Hardcore Castile. Then I heard M-16 weapons fire. I threw the pig back together and we started coming in with caution.

When we got back, we found out that one guy had been blown away. He had been a close-minded southerner, but he had begun to be all right with everybody in the platoon. We knew that he was a racist type of guy—from Arkansas. Matter of fact, I was in his squad once, and I pulled guard duty with him. After we found out that he was OK, we accepted him. He had been lackadaisically walking around and got shot right in the head, in a supposedly safe area, while my men were out having fun, and I was relaxed to the degree that I'd torn down my pig. Again I thought, wow, could have been me. Could have been one of my men. You never knew. You never knew.

One night Doc came around and said, "Hey man, the brigade is looking for a bugler." "A bugler?" "Yeah. Didn't you tell me you played cornet in high school?" "Yeah, I did." "Well, man, they're looking for a bugler—and with what you're up for—I know I could probably go ahead and maybe whisper to the CO, and I think I could get you out of here, man." "Are you kidding?" "No, man." "You would do that for me, man?" "Sure, I'd do it for you." "What do you mean? Wow, Doc, I don't know what to say." He said, "Hey, man, you deserve it, man, you deserve it." At that time I didn't know what he meant by "what I was up for"—even if he had said DSC (Distinguished Service Cross) I wouldn't have known what it was. I was even shocked that a white guy was willing to do this for a black man. He told me to keep it under my hat, anyway. I dared not even tell my best buddy. And I didn't.

The next day, Doc came around giving out his vitamins.

When he got to me, he said, "The CO bought it, man. You're going out of the boonies." "You bullshitting?" He said, "No. Don't say nothing, now." "OK." I was so excited, man, I couldn't even hardly keep still. It was the greatest thing that had ever happened in my life. It was like a guy slated for dying and finds out that he's not going to die—it was like that. The very next day, Doc came round again. It was all whispering. He said, "OK—now, there's going to be a chopper—" I wasn't to tell *anybody*. I really hated that. That was the only sad thing about it all; I couldn't tell anybody. I knew the brothers were going to think I blown them out or some shit. That was what I was thinking in my own mind—wow, I couldn't tell anybody. Look what the implications were—I was deserting them! What the fuck was wrong with me? Anybody out here would do the same fucking thing. Just go out and blow a bugle. It wasn't that I was getting out of the war, but going to be a bugler—and I might not even make it. They were telling me there were going to be forty guys participating. The sergeant major had sent word around to all of the battalions in the American division, I was told, and that was a lot of battalions. Doc told me, "Man, you might be out of here fifteen days, thirty days; the thing about it is that you are out, man, and when you get back there, when they know what you're up for, you probably won't be back." I didn't believe him. I thought, shit, if I didn't blow the hell outa this bugle, I was fucked. But it was a chance, you know.

Then Doc came and said, "Your taxi is going to be the hot food chopper but remember, keep it under your hat. Don't you say anything. You just start walking for that chopper, you understand? You don't have to say goodbye. You don't have to nod to the CO. Just walk toward that fucking chopper. Just like that." Oh man, it was like you were being channeled out of there, you know. And that was what it was, too. I told Emory. I didn't walk off from Emory. Emory was always right by me. He knew it even before Piper knew it. I wasn't thinking white or black; I had to tell men that allied themselves with me, like Emory. And if I told him, I just could not leave the field without telling my black compadres. I just could not do that. That was why I told all the guys that were closest to me. There was no way that I was going to leave the boonies having white guys—Emory and Doc—know.

You couldn't think just white or just black—you had to think for everybody. That was one of the things that the war did for me. It started me thinking about men in general, instead of whites or blacks—even though a lot of the whites forgot about that after they got back to the states. It taught them a lot of lessons. Some whites never forgot it. And a lot of blacks never forgot it either.

Piper was bullshitting with me, and I said, "Hey, man." "Yeah, man, what's going on, man?" "I'm leaving." "You're what?" "Yep, I'm leaving. Hush now, don't say nothing, I'm not supposed to tell anybody." I was looking all down at the ground, looking all around, you know. And he said, "You're leaving?" I said, "Yeah. That chopper that's bringing our hot chow is going to be the one that I'm going to leave on." "You're bullshitting. Who else knows this, man?" I said, "Nobody but you. Don't tell nobody man until I'm on the chopper." "I'm happy for you, man." But I could see he was sort of hurt. It should have been him, right? Then it dawned on me why the Doc didn't want me to tell nobody. Piper was one of ten guys that had been out in the boonies longest, for maybe seven or eight months. Then I saw the hurt in his eyes, but he didn't say nothing. Every time he looked at me, he'd just look at me longingly. Sort of shook his head. I thought, wow, he was taking it hard. I'd be lucky to reach this chopper; I should have kept my mouth shut. It occurred to me that if the wrong guy found out, I could have another berserk guy on my hands.

When the chopper came the guys took it beautifully. I remember Belt; he knew I was leaving because Piper had told him. These guys were tight. They admired me because I told them. I didn't have to tell anything. On the one hand, they could take it and respect me because I'm black and I was getting a chance to get out of this war. And then again, it could mean that black didn't matter, especially because of the other guys. I was just a man that was going out of the war, and "it should be me." But they took it that a black man got his chance to leave this war in one piece, not hurt or anything. As I started walking by, Belt said under his breath, "Bye, Goff." It was very sad; here I was, picked out of all these guys to go. Any one of them was good enough to go. Any of them. I can't ever really give you the feeling of what I felt as I walked by those guys—tears were in my eyes. They all saw me walking toward the chopper, and some of the guys said, "Where you going, man?" And then it dawned on them: this guy was getting out of the boonies. They knew I was up for the citation. As I was walking toward the chopper, I heard "You forgot to say bye, God damn it." It was Hardcore. I just turned around and waved to him. Then the chopper was on the ground. I saw the CO. He looked at me. I dared not wave to him; you weren't supposed to do that shit, so I just looked at him. Then I looked at Doc. He was looking at me. It looked as though he was proud of me. He was smiling. I looked at him and thought, that was my man right there. That was my ticket. How could I ever repay that Doc? To this day I would just love to know where that man is. His name is Doc, is all I know. As I got farther and farther away, I couldn't stop looking at those men in the boonies. They didn't want to keep staring at me. It just hurt them too much. They all turned around and stared back down at the ground.

Bob

9 C COMPANY

Until my unit pursued the enemy into the mountains around Dalat, 3d Battalion of the 173d worked the area around Bao Loc in the southern part of II Corps. Bao Loc became a familiar locale to Charlie Company. We came in for four days in-country R & R after every operation but it wasn't like we came in for a vacation. We came to rest, but we rested by pulling perimeter guard day and night. The guys originally on guard just moved back into the center of the compound. We were alternating with the rest of the battalion; when B Company came in for a rest, then we went out; when we went out, D Company came in. When the companies had to be in the field, then they had "spoons" to guard the perimeter at the fire base. In the field, guys in the rear called us boonie rats, beetle stompers, bush beetles, funky grunts. We called the guys in the rear spoons because they were the cooks and dishwashers for the colonels and other officers that stayed in the rear area. They had a regular mess hall back in the rear. It was a big old tent, like a circus tent. The spoons worked there. The rear echelon never went to the field for anything. All they did was sort the mail that came in from Saigon or the APO and stayed back cooking and washing pots. Sometimes they would load the choppers to bring out the ammo and the mail.

The spoons knew the whole scene on the strip. In the six or seven houses there, the Vietnamese in the village sold any kind of dope you could get. They sold bootleg whiskey, half–diluted coca cola and warm beer. Piss beer, I called it, but it was better than nothing after eighty or ninety days in the field. After humping, piss beer tasted good. They didn't have no refrigerators, so they kept it in a cool dry area down underneath the floor boards of their shacks. They would hide it in case the MPs came in to check out what was happening.

When we would come out of the field, we'd want some boom–boom, a piece of tail. We weren't allowed to go to the strip, but we'd slip out of the compound and try to look for women. Since we were part of the perimeter guard, we'd make us a hole in the fence and would patch it up later. Everybody had their turns at slipping out. During the three or four days that we were in the rear, we were only responsible for our part of the perimeter. Hell, the guys on the other side could get out any way they could and get theirs. We'd always leave enough guys on guard. It was quiet in the daytime, and we never slipped out at night. It was not only risky, but it was possible to get our ass burnt. Who knew when we were coming back in; who knew if that wasn't Charlie trying to sneak in there?

You had to have a little bit of those things that made you feel good. We got some hot slop, something to drink; we got some boom–boom. Really, man, those were the things that you lived for. That was the only thing that kept us going out in the field.

The conditions in Vietnam made dealing with Charlie very difficult. No one ever mentioned anything in training about what Vietnam would be like. We went through all that training, and they never did mention the elements or the leeches. The only thing they said was that Vietnam was hot. Oh sure, they mentioned malaria–carrying mosquitos. I remember one sergeant told us about the bamboo vipers. He said one of the favorite tricks of the Vietnamese was to use the vipers on the trails. When they knew you were coming up the trail, they'd tie the viper along the trail with a vine or a little string. Maybe they'd whip him or something. By the time you got there, he'd be really pissed, and he'd nip you on the neck. We heard that the Vietnamese would put them in the doorway of a hootch. As soon as you opened the door and walked in, one would fall down from where they had rigged it and maybe nip you. These snakes were about ten or twelve inches long and were one of the most poisonous snakes in Vietnam. You were supposed to be dead within ten seconds after they hit you. They were hard to see, too. They had different colors — green, brown, greenish-brown, and one with black and white stripes. That was supposed to be the deadliest snake of all. We saw quite a few around the thick bamboo areas, but I didn't see any that were booby-trapped.

The NCOs prepared us for booby traps. They said, "Don't pick up souvenirs." In other words, if you saw a cigarette lighter or something laying on the ground, it probably was a booby-trap. If you saw an old Vietnamese weapon blown to smithereens, naturally you would want to pick it up to bring home. But it could have been attached to an antipersonnel mine. I didn't see any snake booby traps, but I did see quite a few of the other kind.

What bugged me most of all was when they used to give us a little bottle of insect repellant. They'd give us one maybe every two or three weeks. And we'd use that thing up in one hour. Or it might last until we hit the water in the swamps or until the monsoon hit us. It was maybe 110 degrees above the treelines. Down below, where we were in the underbrush, it seemed to be that hot all the time.

We would be walking in an inch and a half of mud and muck. The leeches were on top of the mud. They were not those two-inch long water leeches. We saw a few of them, but we never had problems with those. These were the little brown leeches, little bloodsuckers. They could smell you out from ten feet away, and before you knew it, you were grabbed by them. You could actually look on the ground and sometimes, if the area were really infested, you could see at least a hundred coming your way. And there'd be another hundred going towards your buddy. The trouble was, you could never feel them, except when they would get so full of blood that they would begin to drop off. If you were walking in an infested area, you'd try to put your pant legs down inside your boots. You'd try to lace your boots around your pants real tight; it would even cut off the circulation, it would be so tight, just to keep them out. But they would come through the little lace holes of your shoes and just crawl all the way up the back or front of your pants heading for the very warm areas under your armpit and in your crotch. In fact, I had a partner that had one crawl right in the hole at the head of his penis. The only way to get it out was to operate. The leech is about a quarter of an inch in length, so skinny, he looked like a broomstraw when he started in on you. When he finished, he'd be about two inches long and about half an inch in diameter. After he got full of blood, he'd just drop off of you. And when he dropped, he left the head in. That was how you knew he'd been there; you felt the sting and a lump underneath there that didn't belong. You'd take a cigarette and burn him off because you couldn't just pull him off. I was sharing more cigarettes with the leeches than I was smoking.

What really bothered me, though, was that I could not understand how the Vietnamese could make it. They would be out there in these little showershoes, no boots, no repellant, no nothing. I would think that the leeches would be all over them because they had so much skin exposed. I guess the leeches never did bother them, but they were hard on me. When the point man would spot something and you got down, that was when those little bloodsucking mothers would come for you. Man, I'm not exaggerating; I have had more than a hundred leeches on me at one time. And I couldn't touch them. My total concentration was on Charlie; I could kill the leeches later. You might be right next to a snake. When the point man signalled that "HALT," you halted!

We used to have a saying: "If I die I'm going to Heaven because I'm already in Hell right here." We were getting various diseases—malaria, hepatitis, trichomoniasis. I got sick from drinking the swamp water. They used to give us water purification tablets. They were little pills that you dropped in your canteen when you filled it. Even though the water was muddy when you first got it, the pill was supposed to clear it up, but, half the time you wouldn't have any of those pills. Even if you had them, during the monsoon, you would be so saturated they would just dissolve right in your pocket or wherever you had them. You wouldn't have time for that, anyway. According to the company commander, we were to "Keep moving, keep your mouth shut, watch the trails, cut that bush and keep pushing." In other words, "Drive On." Trichomoniasis is caused by a little john–type bug that gets in your bladder. It would cause itching around the penis area, and maybe you'd break out with tiny bumps. It could be cured. They gave us some pills that should clear it right up. But it was very uncomfortable. They wouldn't take you out of the field for anything like that. In fact, we had guys out there who went through operations with toothaches. They had bad teeth, so tough shit. You think they were going to bring a chopper out there to get you for a toothache? They were pulled the same day that we went back to the field— and that was that! They didn't care about small things.

The medics did their best. Those field medics, man, they busted their ass. They had 120 people to take care of. They had their own pack on their back, plus they had to carry all their medical equipment. They did a fantastic job. We were cutting an LZ, and I cut my finger half off with a machete; the joint was just hanging on. The medic patched it up, man, and a month later the finger was as good as new. The medic could help a little, but the elements were bad and the enemy was an

ass-kicker. What made it rough was the combination. I hated
the leeches; I hated the monsoon. But the main thing I hated
was just being there!

We never had peace of mind, never had time to relax. If it
wasn't one thing, it was another. It was a nightmare. We had a
saying about when we relaxed and started half-stepping:
"When you half-step, it may be your last step." The enemy
never fought us until he was ready to deal with us. That was
what was so scary about it. He knew exactly where we were at
all times. He was such a master of camouflage that he could be
ten feet away from us and we'd never know it. He used all types
of diversion and tricks. He would dig what we called spider holes.
We'd be walking right on top of the enemy. As soon as he felt
the last guy come through, or if the brush was so thick that the
guy in back of you couldn't tell what was happening, within
a split second he'd raise right out of the ground and just bust
you in the back of the head with a single shot weapon. Then
he'd be right back down in the ground, and you didn't even
know where the shot came from. You'd be looking in the trees
or in the bush next to you, and he'd be back down in the ground,
maybe moving to a different location. He was good. "Sir
Charlie," that was what we called him.

We respected Charlie. And we had some self-respect, too.
Half the guys didn't want to be there in the first place; the other
half didn't know what the hell was going on. But since we were
all there, we didn't just want to give up the ghost, man. It got
to be a challenge. Not a gung ho type of thing, but it got to the
point that if they wanted to try and kick our ass, we'd deal with
it. We believed we could beat anybody.

The American soldier is sort of funny. He's the laziest joker in
the world. He'll kick back any time he can. But when his back is
against the wall, then he becomes the best in the world. Whenever we would get in a fire fight, we felt we could take care of
Charlie, just put him away, if we had to. To me it was a strange
feeling to even shoot anyone. But whenever we got hit, most of
the people took care of business. We all tried to get some

scunnions out there on Charlie's ass, to get him back off of us. And that was our main feeling.

For the first time in my life, I saw total unity and harmony. In the states, even in the rear in Nam, blacks and whites fought each other. But in the Nam, man, out in the field we were just a force of unity and harmony. We became just one person. When I first got to the Nam, I saw a lot of prejudice and shit like that. But Charlie had a tendency to make you unify in a hurry. After he started kicking your ass, your anger and your common sense told you that you needed everybody. I mean EVERYONE. That was because a few people could get the whole company killed in just a matter of seconds if they were not doing their job, if they were not sharing in trying to counter Charlie when he attacked. This was something you learned. The army couldn't make you understand. Naturally they told you, "You're a fighting team." You became a machine. You stuck together and you did everything together. You didn't have time for philosophizing. After a while, you saw it; you felt it; you became a part of it.

Sometimes it takes tragedy to bring people together. It really does. And I can't think of anything more tragic than that situation at that time. Little things happened. Guys ran out of cigarettes; they shared. We ran out of food during the monsoon up in the mountains. Whoever had any salt left or a little cocoa, maybe a package of coffee, shared it. That one little package of coffee went around to four or five guys. By the time it got to you, the coffee looked like tinted water, but it was something liquid. Being in a hell hole just automatically brought every guy together as one. It was a good feeling. That was the only thing that was good about Vietnam, as far as I'm concerned. For the first time in my life, I saw people as people. We was just us, you know, man, it was US.

The Vietnamese constantly appealed to blacks to get out of the war. They would leave leaflets laying all over the jungle. In perfectly good English, the leaflet would say, "Blacks get out, it's not your fight," or, "They call us gooks here and they call

you niggers over there. You're the same as us. Get out, it's not
your fight." In some ways those leaflets affected morale. It
would make us wonder why we were there. Most of the people
were like me; they were naive. We didn't know what the hell
was really going on. We knew that Communists were supposed
to be bad, and that they were trying to take the South Vietnamese's rice away from them, and that we were out there to
stop them. But at the same time, the Black Panther organization, the Muslims, the Kings didn't feel that we should be out
there participating in it. We didn't have nothing to gain from
being there. We felt that if we were drafted we had a duty to go
to war because we were Americans. But coming home reminded
us that going was no benefit to us. Ho Chi Minh made a point
that stuck in many of our minds. He said, "It's a civil war. The
war is between the Vietnamese, between the North and the
South." He made the point that "when you had your North and
your South, or your Blue and your Gray, we didn't drop bombs
in San Francisco, we didn't attack New York. So why should
you be dropping bombs on Hanoi or Haiphong or all over
Vietnam? If you was to get out, we'd settle our own differ-
ences." Old Ho Chi made sense to most of us. This kinda idea
especially made sense to me, because we had too many Americans dying. And it was obvious that we were the aggressors
because we were fourteen thousand miles from home rather
than vice versa. We were fighting Charlie in his own backyard.
We didn't really feel that we were fighting for our country; half
the brothers felt it wasn't even our war and were sympathetic
with Ho Chi Minh.

When I was in the Nam, Mohammed Ali was refusing to take
the oath. Our reaction was that we shouldn't have taken it
either. We felt that the American Dream didn't really serve us.
What we experienced was the American Nightmare. Black
people were fighting with honor in Vietnam just like they did in
other American wars. They never ran; they fought to the death.
We felt that they put us on the front lines abroad and in the
back lines at home. Most of the brothers felt the same, even

though we fought right along. We wouldn't give up. We did
our best to keep trucking out there and in the woods, but we
would always think about this. We used to sit down and have
talks over it. We'd say, "What the fuck are we doing in Vietnam, man? When we get back to the states, we gonna be treated
shitty and funky, anyway." So I could understand where these
brothers were coming from. We felt that blacks should not have
had to fight in Vietnam if, when they got home, they couldn't
even get a job. We had unity and harmony because we wanted
to live. But we just wanted no part of the war. I know I didn't.
The benefits were just not there for us. Martin Luther King was
saying this stuff when he got killed. We talked about King and
Malcolm. King was a preacher, and we said, "If they kill a
preacher, what are they going to do to us, even though we're
over here fighting for them?" It was the hypocritical part of all
the talk of the war that bothered me.

Another thing that got me was the South Vietnamese. We
were in Vietnam helping them and they would try to beat us out
of the little money we had. I felt that they exploited the GIs.
Plus they wouldn't help us fight. We never did see the regular
South Vietnamese army in the field. They would be guarding
the bridges or be hidden away in some compound somewhere.
When we could come into contact with them, we'd have fist
fights. We would call them lazy asses. We used to have run-ins
with them all the time. We were fighting for them and they
were scared to fight for themselves. They used to pick up and
run. They would always shy away from fighting at night. They
wouldn't even fight for their own country; we didn't see any
reason why we should. We would be out in the field so long,
we would have battle fatigue. Man, it was just a hassle for us.
The ARVN would have the best made U. S. weapons and their
weapons would stay shiny because they never used them. All
they did was profile with them. It was like they weren't even in
the war, because we took it over for them.

But I have to say one thing. Charlie himself—the North Vietnamese soldier—was tough, man. I mean, they really got down

to it. What frightened me most of all was that it was a political war. Charlie had a philosophy; they'd say that we were aggressors, that we shouldn't have been there interfering in their affairs. To me, it seemed like it was between North and South Vietnam. It was sort of like a revolution they were fighting. A lot of Vietnamese didn't want us there. They didn't need anyone interfering. They believed that to the bone, that one grain of rice was worth one drop of blood. And many times, when you would kill an enemy, you could see they were little kids out there fighting you. Or women. Actually see them laying there dead. I would wonder what provoked a woman or a little kid to get out there and fight like this unless they honest to God felt that their beliefs were right. It was scary to me, waking me up, making me ask what I was doing there. I mean, what WERE we doing there? We weren't supposed to know anything or say anything—just keep taking orders and moving along. But still I had my own mind. I still had to think for myself about what I was fighting for. I felt that if war broke out on the shores of America, hell, I'd fight my heart out. But we were half a world away. I couldn't see that we were accomplishing anything.

We'd take one hill, we'd lose a lot of dead, there'd be a lot of bloodshed. And then, the next thing I'd know, we were gone from this hill. A couple of months later, we had to go back and take the same hill again. We were just out there walking and looking. And it seemed like we were going in circles, and sometimes we would be exposed right out in the middle of rice paddies where the NVA or the VC could set up an ambush and kill or maim some of us. We talked about it every day. All the guys felt the same way. We just weren't accomplishing anything. In fact, some guys were so depressed and disgusted that they was killing themselves. Some guys were taking hand grenades and blowing themselves away. They couldn't stand the strain anymore. It was really heavy. I don't think a lot of this stuff was reported. Guys would just kill themselves, and the army would probably send the stats home that the guys was killed or missing in action. Maybe even proclaim them heroes. Hell, I felt everybody out there was a hero. I hated to see a guy blowing himself away. But guys couldn't take it any more. And it happened all over Vietnam. Guys going crazy; I mean losing it mentally. Some guys got so fatigued and so screwed up in their minds, they would start firing up in the sky, firing anywhere.

Bob

10 DALAT TO PHAN RANG

By this time Stan was out of the field for good, but I didn't know it then. My unit was still chasing the Vietnamese that had wiped out B Company. We began to move into the big tea plantations in the Dalat area, down at the foot of the mountains, between Dalat and Phan Rang, on the coast. The tea plantations were just acres and acres of this really green, stumpy bush. There were long rows of tea bushes about three feet high. The farmers would be out there cultivating it during the day. Right at the end of the tea plantation would usually be a little Vietnamese village. There were some old French houses, too. They were like American houses, but most of them were run down with the windows torn out of them. I guess the people moved out a long time ago. At the edges of the plantation there were tree lines, also heavy brush, and it was all overgrown. That was where we could be ambushed.

The entire battalion was working in the general area of the tea plantations and up into the mountains above them. Each company was maybe fifteen miles apart: Charlie Company on one side of a mountain; Bravo Company on the other side; Alpha Company down below; and Delta Company up above. Whenever one company would get hit bad, then they would call the helicopters, and they'd bring another over to give them a hand. It was up one mountain, down a gorge, back up another mountain. Sometimes we would go for three or four days at a time before we would run into contact. When that happened, it seemed like the Vietnamese knew exactly when we were tired. They would just wait it out.

The noise discipline wasn't secure. Guys would be cursing all over the place. The monsoon hit us on our way toward Dalat. We'd be climbing up the hill and get almost to the top and it would be real slippery. We could slip all the way back down about fifty feet. Your rucksacks would be ripped to shreds by the time we hit bottom. We had to fix all that back up together and then catch up with the rest of the company. Even the company commander would be shouting obscenities all over the place.

I used to walk point every other day. I wanted to walk point because I hated to put my life in another man's hands. Every organization had a few goof-offs, some guys who weren't quite alert. It's important to remember that there was a big turnover all the time, guys coming in, guys going home, or guys getting killed or wounded, and other guys replacing them. There was no way in hell I'd let a new guy walk point for me. They didn't know what they was dealing with. And it wasn't their fault. They just didn't know what was happening. I didn't want to die for that reason, so I used to walk point. It really scared me to walk point, but I got used to it after a while. You never quite got over that fear. The point man led the company. Right in back of him was the man with the compass—to make sure that you stayed on the course that the company commander had designated. Everybody in the company depended on the point man to keep his head together and get us there.

You had to be alert on point at all times. If the point man walked into the killing zone of an ambush, within seven to ten seconds you'd all be dead or dying. If the point man suspected an ambush, he held up the company by making some signal to stop the next man back of him. When the point man stopped, the word went all the way back automatically. We tried to keep about ten-foot intervals between each man. Each man passed the word back.

Sometimes we'd know that Charlie was following us. We knew this because sometimes we had to make a couple of kills as we walked down the trail. The point man might have seen Charlie coming up the trail, so we'd hit him right then and there. Or we'd just walk up on them, as they did get careless sometimes, too. But sometimes as we'd be walking back down the trail to set up an ambush, they would ambush us.

Chasing those Vietnamese units, we'd walk maybe twenty-five miles a day, though it always seemed like a hundred miles. When we wound up near a village, we had to check it out. As we moved up into the mountains, the people there were Montagnard. They had their own villages with pigs, chickens, and corn. When Charlie needed food, whenever he needed resupply, he would just go out and literally take it from the village. We had helicopters bringing us food when we ran out. Sometimes Charlie would have the villagers running errands for him. He'd hide what he couldn't carry in some of the villages, because he was moving around. We'd go into these villages, and many times we'd find caches buried in the ground—enough corn to feed maybe two thousand people. When we went into the villages, we'd tear down sheds, look underneath the floor boards of the Vietnamese houses. Sometimes we'd find little trap doors and inside there'd be a cache.

These people were sympathizers either voluntarily or by force. Most of the time it was by force. Charlie would come in, take the village chief, and just cut his guts out right there. He'd make an example for the rest of the people in the village, maybe by crucifixion. We took some of these people down; I have actually seen where they slaughtered them. We found people that were terrified, caught in the middle. They didn't want to be part of either side. The company commander and the Vietnamese interpreters, whom we called cowboy scouts, would get them off to the side and try to interrogate them. But they wouldn't tell us much. Then we'd start to go through the village, checking it out. As far as we knew, we might have been talking to some of the enemy.

As we went into the village, we would set up a perimeter and run patrols in all four directions out of the village to make sure that there were no ambushes set up for us. In the meantime, the company commander would call in Chinooks. If they couldn't get in there, they would drop their long drop lines with storage tanks. Then we'd get the corn and other stuff loaded up. We did that a lot. Sometimes we would find weapons. That was when the command would really go in and analyze that village pretty carefully. They would take the village chief and a few other people back to the fire support base, maybe twenty-five or thirty miles away, and interrogate them.

I remember a Montagnard village in the mountains near Dalat. Maybe ten or twelve guys did get shot-happy. They saw somebody running down toward these tunnels, so all hell broke loose. Our troops seemed to be the only ones firing, and people were running, screaming, crying. I saw one old man dead, but I didn't see anybody else killed. Somebody said they thought he was a Viet Cong because he ran. To me, the guy was just running for shelter. That incident puzzled me. Another time we went to a village in the same area where pigs and chickens were killed. But it seemed like these people were harmless. We never did go in and wipe out a whole village. Our company commander was a righteous person; he didn't allow that at all. We Americans weren't supposed to fire on a village where there were civilians, even if we got incoming rounds. Now, I never thought that was right. If we were walking through a village and somebody started shooting at us, we weren't supposed to shoot at all? What the hell were we supposed to do? Stand there and die? That was stupid!

When the South Koreans were there, they didn't have to get one round coming out of the village. If they suspected that there was NVA in the village, they would kill everyone in that village. Everyone! And I have seen villages they went through. We would read and hear how they mopped up everything, like a tornado. They went through, killing everybody and everything. They were some mean dudes, brutal. A lot of things they did were uncalled for. We didn't have nothing to do with that, but the command of the 173d actually worked with the Korean White Horse Division.

Anytime we made contact and there were some dead, there might be mutilation, but I don't know if the Koreans or Charlie actually started it. They would do a lot of things to instill fear, the psychological effect being the main motive. The enemy did anything he could to intimidate you or make you go crazy. And some guys did go crazy.

We had one guy who jumped down on his own frag and blew himself away. Another partner shot himself right through the groin. They had to ship him back to the World. I'm not saying their psychology was directly causing the suicides and self-mutilation, but I think it had a lot to do with it.

Say, for instance, Charlie hit a unit. The village that supported him was completely blown away by the Koreans. He'd be mad as hell. Since he knew where you were, he tried to hit you when he had a real advantage. He never surrendered and he really intimidated us. He would hit one of our companies with a full battalion. Since you'd be outnumbered three or four to one, he would overrun you. Then, before help could arrive, he would go through your pockets, get all the documents, watches and rings. He didn't bother to snip them off our finger. He carried machetes. So he took the finger and cut your head clear off. He'd take your penis or your balls and put them in your mouth. Guys in Company B told us where they cut off a black guy's head and put it on a white guy's body. It was gross, nasty. When Bravo Company of the 3d Battalion of the 503d got mopped up, Charlie mutilated their dead. Here's what guys felt: "If Charlie can do it, then we're going to do the same thing to him if we kill him." All the mutilation did was just piss you off. Charlie turned you into an animal. Psychologically he hurt you, because if you were to do this, then you were no better than he was.

An order from the brigade commander tried to put a stop to mutilations. It said that if mutilating the dead didn't stop, the people associated with it would be court-martialed and would receive dishonorable discharges. So he was saying, "Don't do it. Leave the dead. You must respect the dead. Don't mutilate them; bury them." On the average, most Americans are raised to respect the dead. You don't go cutting them up. So when we made kills, we would actually bury the Vietnamese dead right there. Our dead were shipped back home. But a few guys continued to do it. One guy in particular had a reputation. I never knew his real name, but if anyone was ever in his unit, they'd know him. The story was that he was out in the bush for three years without an R & R. He even refused R & R. This guy was vicious. He used to wear a chain of ears around his neck and along his belt. He was just an animal.

There was a lot of depression going with the constant strain of humping and fire fights. I was really down lots of time, and most of the cats were. "Depressed" is an understatement. We were so down half of the time, we didn't know what we were going to do next, and we didn't care. We lost spirit cause we were just out there humping. Our motto was "Drive On." No matter what happened, no matter what came down, we just drove on, with our ears constantly open.

I couldn't understand the war. I had nothing against President Johnson personally. I just lived under his policy. But I couldn't understand why he halted the bombing in 1968 and left us in the field. It jeopardized my life more than ever. At that time, enemy activity stepped up. We lost more dead and wounded. We believed that the bombing slowed down infiltration, and that it protected us. At the time that the bombing was halted in 1968, it was the heaviest of the war. But we felt the war itself should have been halted. We used to read stuff in the *Pacific Stars and Stripes* about the Paris peace talks and we hoped that they would get in there and negotiate. That way they would pull us out. We didn't feel that we should be left out in the field, because then there was nothing to stop Charlie from coming down in greater numbers. And that was what happened. It seemed like the government supported Charlie more than they did us. We understood that it was politics, but it was not militarily correct. And that was when we got our ass kicked. Prior to the bombing halt, we were making contact once every two weeks, sometimes twice a week at the most. But after the bombing halt, we started making contact every other day, and really heavy contact. We started running into more modern weapons. Every time we looked around, some incoming shit was coming in on our ass, bringing scunnions on people. Some of that bombing might have slowed them up. That shit got really heavy. We were more fatigued than ever. I hadn't had any R & R. It was like every day, every night. They even started hitting us at night. So it was really stinking, I tell you. I made it, but I just wish all the cats could have made it, too. Most of the dudes that died over there had nothing to do with the control of the war. I feel sorry for them.

I remember we got hit on Christmas Day. Prior to going to Vietnam, I read in the newspaper that there was supposed to be a truce, a standdown on Christmas Day and no one was supposed to fight. So it was raining like a bitch. We were getting hit everywhere, and we were so far out in the field that it didn't matter. I was looking for the truce. I said to myself, "Damn, I thought it was supposed to be a truce today." I knew it was a truce because at least they let us know that much. We didn't have time to read no calendar, figure out what day it was. All we were trying to do was to live. When you have a nightmare and you wake up in the morning, you think to yourself, "Geez, I'm glad that was a dream." Well, to me Vietnam was like a nightmare for a whole year without waking up.

Every minute of it I was scared; every night, doubly scared. It
got to the point where I was frightened all the time, and it did
something to me. It shattered my nerves and confidence. Either
it broke you or made you hard. I didn't know if people would
ever be themselves after they experienced something like that—
because it was hell.

When we started moving back into the mountains, the area
around Dalat was getting a lot of heavy contact. Late one afternoon they put us on cattle trucks, and we rode out right into
the night, so we knew it was an emergency. Finally they
brought us into Dalat and we saw dead civilians laying in
the streets, women and babies with people bending over them,
crying. We could smell white phosphorus and human flesh. The
whole city was burning because it was getting mortared and
rocketed. Charlie just took over the city for a moment. He
robbed it of everything, all types of food and supplies. There
was much firing, and we knew that we were dealing with a large
element. We got off the trucks and our entire company took a
position in this huge ditch. We were told that Bravo and Delta
Companies were driving the NVA our way. We were the block-
ing force along this road going through Dalat. We stayed there
two or three hours. Then, all of a sudden, the company commander ordered us to move out to the compound. They brought
us in to be resupplied and to set up a night defensive perimeter.
The compound had been hit earlier. Some of the other companies—Bravo, Delta—were there too as well as some units of
the 25th Infantry from Phan Rang. That next day we checked
out the city to see if the enemy was still lingering on the outskirts of the town. I guess intelligence was trying to find out
where Charlie had gone. That night we swept the city and
moved on into the compound. So the first night when we thought
they would attack, they didn't, but they attacked the compound
the second night.

About eleven o'clock, they started mortaring the compound
from the hillsides, about a thousand of them. Before we knew
it, they were on the ground near the concertina wire. They

started trying to get through, and we was firing at them from bunkers. They were falling and dying all over the concertina. When we would fight them back on one side of the compound, they would try to get in on the other side. All the enemy we captured were wounded.

There must have been thousands of them in the attack. We were fighting constantly until about five o'clock the next morning. They had mortared us most of the night, and their attack came about three or four o'clock. Some of the NVA got through the wire, but they were dead. The next morning bodies were everywhere. They had surrounded the entire compound. They were carrying AK–47s, BARs and 122mm rockets on mop sticks. They were all around the compound, hanging on the concertina. The same unit that had jumped B Company met this larger unit. So they had had their own little Tet Offensive. They were like a raiding party, going around in small bands doing a job on people until they all hooked up. After we dropped a heavy loss on them by beating back their assault, we brought in some more troops—Alpha Company that had been left back in Bao Loc to secure that area.

The morning after the attack, we counted our dead. The medivacs came in and worked on the wounded and took them out. We chowed down and then helped clean up the compound. After the reinforcements arrived, we started to move out of the compound and dispersed in different directions. We took off to search out the remaining NVA that we hadn't killed in the battle. We followed some of them real close. From that time on, for the next two months, we were constantly making contact; we would kill a few of them, and they would kill or wound a few of us. After about two months the fighting tailed off. I can't really be specific on any fire fight because there were so many. We were getting hit every other day. I caught some fragments in my hand and a burn in my right eye, and, of course, everyone had jungle rot.

But none of that was enough to get us out of the field. I didn't want to just leave the field; I wanted to leave to come home, but

I had partners out there, man. Once you get real tight with your friends, no matter what, you hate to leave your partners out there. If I had to be in Vietnam, it was important to be with my friends.

Another time we were high up in the mountains near Dalat. It was during the monsoon, so we couldn't get any resupply. Once the storm set in, the helicopters couldn't land, so we were out of food, twelve days there in the rain. Everything was wet, no chow, nothing. Some dudes were taking the C–4 out of the claymore mines and cooking just regular old weeds and grass and stuff that you pulled up out of the side of the trail. They were putting that in their canteen cups with a little salt and pepper and trying to cook it.

The CO sent out a patrol looking for food and they killed this monkey. When we got him back to camp, we skinned him. I hadn't ever eaten monkey before. Here the guys were saying, "I ain't going to eat none of that God damn monkey." "That's my last resort." "Before I eat some of that monkey, I'd rather starve." We started cooking it, and before you knew it, everybody was in on it. First we tried to roast him on a stick. We tied him up, but some people started to talk about how he was like human meat: "He won't cook good like that. You've got to cook him in a pot." We roasted him to a certain extent; we didn't have no pot. Then we cut little pieces off and started to boil him in our canteen cups. And he was pretty good, although a little rubbery, but I just chewed and swallowed it. I didn't care.

The storm began to let up after about thirteen or fourteen days, and we started to come out of the hills. It wasn't bad enough that we were tired and starving, but we were having to deal with Charlie coming down the hill. We got hit, lost a few dead. Halfway down the mountain the storm stopped, so the choppers came in and picked up the dead and wounded. I thought they were going to airlift us out of there, but they wanted us to continue on down on our way to the fire support base to see if we could make contact. Same old jive! But at least we were going in. They said, "You will be reporting in the next couple of days down to the fire support base where there will be hot showers and mail." Before we made it to the support base, my partner, Ellis, was killed.

Ellis had gone through all that shit in the mountains around Dalat and then died after it was over. We had come down into the tea plantations out of the hills. The operation was over and we were heading for hot showers and hot food. Ellis was a squad leader, a black guy from Carolina, a well-mannered guy, a sergeant E-5. His job was to make sure everyone was functioning as efficiently as possible. Actually, he worked between a squad and platoon because we were so short of leaders.   Anyway, we were working this large tea plantation as we were heading back toward the fire support base. As we were coming out of the plantation, we were finishing up and were all happy and stuff. Everybody kind of lollygagging. One guy in front of Ellis tripped a wire. He was hit in the leg and another guy got hit in the arm. The booby trap blew Ellis' intestines out, just tore him up instantly. That stayed on a guy's mind, because we knew that when we got back to the fire base Ellis was gonna go in. He was getting ready to come home. This shook up a lotta cats. When you got short, man, you hated to go through all that hell, and then turn around and get blowed away with just a few days left. Ellis had been out there for a year minus fifteen days. We felt that he should have been out of the field thirty days prior to going home for no other reason than to clear up the jungle rot and to try to get some of that red dirt out of his skin.

I went on R & R about my ninth month. You could go on R & R six months after you were in Vietnam. Usually most guys went at six months, but I wanted to save mine, so when I came back to the field I wouldn't have that much time left out there. As it turned out, I never did rest up. Most guys were going to Bangkok, Taipei, Singapore, Hong Kong. I'd heard that Bangkok was the best place for women; it was the most popular place for black guys. They brought pictures back of these chicks they rented. So it got to me. I wanted to go someplace like that, too.

But like I say, I was a married man. My wife had been pregnant all the time I was in Vietnam. In September of that year, just before Ellis was killed, I got news my son was born. When they brought out the mail one time in the field, the Red Cross girl came out on the chopper. She gave me the telegram that my wife had sent to Vietnam. The baby was born, he was so many pounds, so many ounces. His name was Robert, Jr. That was on my mind, too. So when my R & R came, I had my chance to see him. I flew to Hawaii to meet my wife. Since I was working for the airlines prior to getting drafted, she flew on one of my passes, which was still in effect. By that time, I really needed a rest.

I caught the supply chopper back to the rear. I had a couple of days to clean up. R & R lasted seven days. They sent me back to An Khe, our home base, and they fitted me up with some clean khakis. The doctor dabbed a little salve on my jungle rot. Then they shipped me back to Cam Ranh Bay; that was the shipping point for all R & Rs. I caught a plane from there to Guam and then flew on to Honolulu. I was glad to get out of Vietnam. I saw real live people besides GIs and didn't have to worry about them shooting at me. Even though I was jumpy and my reactions were different, I tried to play it off. I tried to pretend it wasn't happening. I thought to myself, "God damn, you mean there are people in the world still living civilian–type lives?" I stared at the other people on the flight. We landed in Guam and picked up these civilians. Damn, I was thinking, I was out there in the field, doing all this fighting and shit, and here were people who acted like there wasn't nothing going on at all.

After we landed in Hawaii, they took us over to Fort DeRussy. We sat in this big funky building while they told us what to do, what not to do, when to report back, all this bullshit. "Your quarters are over here." I didn't want any part of the army right then. Especially when they said, "You've got the option of staying on the military installation here, or you can go down to Waikiki Beach. I said, "I'll go to Waikiki, man."

We finally left, and this was the first time I could see my kid, who was getting pretty big. I was really jubilant, overjoyed at seeing the baby, trying to forget about the Vietnam shit. We tried to go see everything in the seven days, taking pictures and running around, but the baby was sick with a cold and getting worse. I took him up to the military hospital and they took care of him. Finally, my time was up; I had to go back. I was one sad motherfucker. I was thinking about going AWOL, man, but I knew I'd never get away with it. I wanted to go home so bad I didn't know what to do, but we said our goodbyes and I headed back to Vietnam.

It seemed like those seven days just jumped, while being in the field a day seemed like a year. Going back to Vietnam was a real downer. I went back the same way I came out—Cam Ranh Bay, then to An Khe, and from An Khe back to my unit. I kept thinking as I was processing back into it, what the fuck was I doing here? Was this me? The first day I got there I thought, this gotta be a dream, man. Vietnam? Me? Was this really me out here? After nine months and my R & R, after being so close to home, I was stunned to be going back. But, I'd seen my baby and that made me feel better. After I rejoined my company, it didn't take me long to adapt because I'd been gone only eight or nine days.

For the next two or three weeks we were just scuffling through the jungle—up one hill and down the next, before we made any contact. It was a good transition back into the boonies. But even if contact came down the first day, I was still ready; it was something you didn't forget. All the leeches, the heat, and all the other shit would put you right back to where you were. But from that time on, I went sour; I didn't want to be there.

If you are doing really tough work, and then if you sit down for a while, you gonna get stiff. And you hate to get back into it. But after you get back into it for a while, you'll be all right. That was how I felt about going back to the Nam.

Stan

11 BUGLER

I knew that getting out of the boonies to become a bugler was a stroke of Fate. As the vibrations of the helicopter had me hanging on, my immediate feeling was that a bullet could still knock me back down to the ground, and I wanted to defeat that at all cost. I just sat there and sort of looked up at the sky and thought, thank you, God. As I sat there, a big grin slowly started easing on my face. I probably grinned the whole trip back. I just couldn't believe it. My first stop was LZ Ross, and as I saw the fire support base coming into view, I thought: well, I had a fight ahead of me to stay out of the boonies. I didn't actually know what was ahead of me. I was still thinking that there were going to be forty guys bucking for that bugler position. If I didn't make it, they'd send me back. Not all the guys applying were in the boonies. I was told that the brigade sergeant major—I mean the sergeant major right up underneath the colonel—sent out a memo to all the battalions in the rear as well as in the field.

As the helicopter neared the ground, I hopped off to look for my company headquarters. It was the first time I'd been back there without my unit, so I was a little lost. Finally I saw "Bravo Company Supplies" on a little tacked-on sign right up on top of a sandbagged bunker built into the side of the hill.

I went in and said to the sergeant, "I'm coming back to the rear to compete for a bugler position. I was ordered out of the field by the brigade sergeant major." He said, "Bugler? No God damn bugler around here. What the hell are you talking about? You got malaria or something?" He was actually serious. I think he thought I really was not in my right mind. "Bugler? There's no bugler out in the boonies. Where the hell you think you are, in the damn states?" "No," I said, "I'm not kidding. I was actually picked out of the field to come in, to try out for a bugler position." "Bugler," he said. "I don't know anything about it. Who told you to come out of the field? What unit are you with?" I told him what company I was with. Then he said, "Who gave you orders to come out of the boonies like that?" I said, "Captain Milpas, my CO." "Awright," he said, "fine. Go over there and sit down, and I'll be right with you." He went back into the hootch and radioed some place; wanted to talk with somebody to verify my story. When he came back, he said, "You Goff?" I said, "Yep." He said, "All right. Listen, I won't be able to get you off today." I didn't ask to where. Hell, I didn't know where I was going, anyway. "Tomorrow morning, though, you be out on the landing strip at eight o'clock. In the meantime, your company is in the first row of hootches just right down the road there, understand?" I said, "OK, fine." I ambled on down the road toward the B Company hootches.

I met a few of the guys, but I didn't tell them anything about what I was doing, because I didn't want to go through that bull-shit any more. I was a little nervous anyway, thinking this shit could filter out at any damn time. Any sergeant could tell me, "I don't know anything about this at all. You're getting your ass back out there the first chopper goes out to your unit." So I said to myself, "Man, you better be cool, just relax—just sort of blend in here like you're part of the units that are already up here." So that's what I did. Guys would see me, and I'd just say, "Hey, man, what's happening?" They'd ask me why I was there, and I'd say, "Aw, I just came in. I don't feel too well . . ."

That night was a typical night in the rear. I pulled guard duty with the rest of the guys. But when eight o'clock came around, I was up there sitting on the landing spot for the supply choppers. The sergeant came down. He said, "Goff, you're going to LZ Baldy, and when you get there, just ask for first sergeant of headquarters company."

I thought LZ Ross was huge, but I never saw anything like LZ Baldy. It was like another big city. It was brigade headquarters, that was why. I couldn't even see the other side of it. I started immediately walking up toward B-TOC (Brigade Tactical Operations Center).

I walked inside and asked for the first sergeant. I met a specialist-4 that talked sort of funny, like he was gay. When I said, "Hey, I want to see the first sergeant," he hesitated, "Uh, the first sergeant . . ." I thought, oh no. He said, "Well, the first sergeant can't see you right now." I said, "OK, fine. Listen, I'll be out here in the front, and you might tell him, Goff is here. OK?" "Here? Here from where?" I said, "Here from LZ Ross by way of Bravo Company. I'm applying for the bugler position." "Bugler position?" This was beginning to get to me, everybody thinking it was so strange, like I was a man from Mars or something. Anyway, I went on out front and sat. I sat there most of the morning. I was getting awfully hungry because I was used to eating C-rations whenever I wanted to eat. One thing about the army, they let you eat. Finally I went back in the office. "Where's the chow, man? Can I go down there and eat?" "Oh, yes. There's no problem." And he told me how to get to the messhall. I left my rucksack and went down. It seemed strange to me — a messhall actually built off the ground. I walked in there and discovered they actually had another area where the guys could eat inside a cafeteria. I found that strange, too. This was beginning to be a little fancy. I'd been out of the boonies only two days after all the weeks of jungle. The guys were looking at me sort of weird. They were all relaxed, and I didn't fit in too well. The chow was pretty good. After I dumped my plate, I went back to the headquarters company.

Finally, the first sergeant appeared. He was a big fat guy, about six feet, two inches; he was sort of a scowly looking person. He said kinda funny, "Are you the bugler? I'm First Sergeant Dove. The brigade sergeant major is not quite ready to see you yet. He's been tied up all day. So I don't know whether you'll see him today or not. In the meantime, you see that tent right there? That'll be your home. You go in there and find yourself a cot and just relax. Right now, I don't have anything else to tell you, so just sort of relax." That was it. And I thought, wow, nobody telling me that I had duty to pull, no KP, no latrine duty, no guard duty, no nothin. Just relax. I just knew I'd be sent down to some infantry company. I had nothing to do. So I just went over there and picked out a cot.

I thought I was going to be shown where the other forty guys were supposed to gather for the competition. I thought I was immediately going to see the sergeant major, and I was going to be on trial that day. If I didn't make it, I was going to go right back out in the boonies. By the end of the day, I was still just sitting there, looking at the twelve empty cots inside this tent. When the guys started drifting in, I occasionally looked up, but I didn't say hi or anything. The only thing I did was lay on that cot and sleep. I'd wake up, then I'd sleep some more.

I got up bright and early. I was the first guy in the mess hall. As I ate, I kept thinking, well, today would probably be THE day. I was just about as excited with this as I was when I got ready to go across that rice paddy; just that keyed up. Everybody was saying, "Good morning." My friend was telling everybody who I was: "Oh, that's the bugler. There's supposed to be about forty other guys, but he's the only guy here." By now everybody thought it was a big joke, and I was laughing, too.

Nothing really happened that morning. Nine o'clock rolled around. Ten o'clock. Nothing happened. Eleven o'clock—God damn, what were they doing? Was I going to meet the sergeant major or wasn't I? Did the top major exist or what? Nothing happened. I just sat there all day in this hot tent, nothing to do, no job assignment. Not that I really wanted to work, but I couldn't understand all this looseness. But what was I worrying about? Other guys would have been just crazy with happiness with nothing to do. But I was climbing the walls. One o'clock came around. I went inside the headquarters company and said, "Hey, sergeant. Am I going to see the sergeant major or what?" So he says, "Look—I don't know, Goff. Right now, I haven't got any word from the sergeant major." I said, "Does the sergeant major know that I'm here, Top?" He said, "The sergeant major knows you're here, Goff." I said, "Where are the rest of the guys?" He said, "I don't know. I don't know any more than you do. Just relax." I heaved one of those big sighs. Then I walked out of the place.

At the end of the second day, the first sergeant came out to me. "Hey, Goff, brigade sergeant major is going to see you tomorrow morning and by the way," he paused, "I heard about you. That was great." I sort of looked down at the ground and said, "Thanks a lot, Top." He went back in his office. And from then on, I could tell, there was a new type of awareness from the men who were around me. I hoped they wouldn't start staring, because that used to embarrass me. I didn't want the guys to treat me special. I didn't really know the significance of being up for a DSC.

From that point on I had full cooperation. I guess we all realized that it probably would take the brigade sergeant major to tell us why, all of a sudden, only one guy showed up and that was me.

Later that night I heard there was a movie for some of the infantry guys that had just gotten in that night. I thought, infantry, my comrades! It was like I knew those guys. I felt comfortable with them. The guys up there at headquarters company had it made so long that I didn't feel comfortable with them at all. They were a different type of guy from the infantry.

I almost trotted to get down where this company was. It might
have been my company. But it wasn't. I saw all these strange
faces—almost all black. I sat down and just blended in with
them. I heard all these war stories while the movie was going
on—"Yeah man, that dude really got it bad, man—I sure hate
the fucking . . . " My face fell because I started thinking that
they could be my company. My own guys could be getting the
shit beat out of them. But finally, after talking about the bad,
then they started talking about the good. They started bullshitting, and that made me feel good, too. I was sitting there
and laughing with them. They started cracking jokes on each
other, playing the dozens with each other. It brought back old
times. Three days out of the boonies and I was going crazy already, missing the guys. But did I want to go back out there?
No way!

After the movie I went down and got some beer. I was trying
to see if maybe I knew anybody from AIT that was in their unit.
But I didn't see anybody that I knew. I sort of felt lonely again,
with nobody to talk to. Once you were in those cliques, it was
like you needed to feel you belonged. Even though I'm black,
they still didn't know me. These guys broke bread together,
starved together out there in the boonies, seen each other's
blood run—so you didn't walk up to them and say, "Hey, man,
what's happening?"

The next morning, sure enough, the Top came over as I was
going to breakfast and told me to be at B–TOC at eight o'clock
to see the sergeant major. I went up to this huge command
headquarters about ten minutes beforehand. B–TOC was a
huge bunker, as big as a house, but it wasn't more than ten feet
off the ground. I walked in and saw pictures on the wall, em-
blems, probably of different units, pictures of different commanders. I stiffen up every time I go by an office. I knew not to
salute, but I was still a little edgy. I was in the rear. I didn't
know what the policies were. By this time I was getting a little
fuzzy in the head.

One major came up to me and said, "Can I help you there,

soldier?" I said, "I'm looking for the brigade sergeant major."
I heard a big resounding voice say, "Right back here, Goff."
The sergeant major was just a picture of military. His fatigues
were immaculate. Every crease was in, and his boots were spit-
shined. Jesus, it looked like you could see yourself in them. He
had a jutting chin, blue eyes, and a shaved head. He looked as
if he stayed in shape, but he was slightly older than I expected,
probably about fifty-five. But he was really sharp. He smiled
and said, "So—you're Goff." I said, "That's right, sergeant
major." I swallowed hard and looked at him. He said, "Well,
first of all, I just want to tell you, you did one hell of a job."
"Uh, thank you very much, sergeant major, I appreciate that."
He said, "Now, let's talk about what I want you to do." He was
standing there with his arms crossed and one leg sort of up
against the wall, eyeing me up and down. "Now what can you
do?" I said, "I don't know what you mean, what can I do, sergeant major." He said, "Well, I know what you can do with a
weapon, Goff, but back here . . . " He moved up and put his
hand on my shoulder. "Back here," he said, "I'm going to give
you a different weapon. I want you to use your head."

I looked at him—jeez, where was he coming from? He said,
"Now, did you type in school?" "No, I'm afraid not, sergeant
major." At that point my feelings were down. "Well, you came
to blow the bugle, right?" I said, "That's it!" Then we both
laughed. He said, "No question about that. But I can't have you
going around here just blowing the bugle, Goff. I'll tell you all
about what I want out of the bugle in a minute. But I've got to
find you another job. You're not going to blow the bugle
twenty-four hours a day, you know. So I gotta find you an
assignment." "Yes, I realize that, sergeant major." "OK," he
said, "now you can't type—hm. Well, I'll come up with something. Don't worry. In the meantime, this is what I want you to
do. Here's my idea of why I'm looking for a bugler. You see,
back here, Goff, we don't see any of the action that you see out
there. These guys don't get a chance. All these guys have got
clerical jobs to do. You know what I mean? So they're getting

a little relaxed. I'm going to put some spit and polish back here. That's what I'm going to do. You understand what I mean, Goff?" "Sure, sergeant major, I understand." "I want a reveille call to wake them up in the morning and a call to put them to sleep. There's a tape. I'm going to have you go back to Chu Lai and meet the bugler there. I'll have your orders cut back to Chu Lai, and there you are to meet the division bugler. I've been trying to get that tape, and I keep putting it off. Every time I go back there, damn it, I forget it. So I want you to take that tape. I want you to listen to it and learn every one of those calls perfectly. I want every one of those calls memorized, OK?" I said, "All right, sergeant major, I'll do it." He said, "OK, fine. In the meantime, I'll come up with a job assignment for you. Goff, you did one hell of a job out there. One hell of a job!" "Thank you very much, sergeant major. Thank you very much." "OK. That'll be all, Goff." He looked after me with his jutting chin as I walked out of his office. That was the last I saw of him.

I got all the way down the hill and thought Damn! what a guy. This guy was really the army. This was the first time I'd seen someone have this much power, this type of control, this type of military expertise. I was in awe: I'll admit it. I was only nineteen years old, not even twenty. This sergeant major was like the president of the United States himself. Me being a black, too. I haven't had white men come up to me and tell me I'd done something great. I was like a kid barely out of high school. I'd been working all my life, but with my hands, bus boy, pot washer, gas pumper. Then, all of a sudden, somebody with authority was throwing me into a different light. I walked back down the hill, and I went, whew! Going up inside of that place and facing all those guys was like running across that rice paddy. I had wanted to say, "Fuck it, I ain't going in there, but damn, I pulled it off. I'm not going back to the boonies." I walked back to my hootch and sort of sat there trying to let off steam. I was still thinking, whew, at least I got a few more days out of this damn thing. Then it started dawning on me.

Chu Lai, I was going to Chu Lai, man. Wow, I hadn't been to Chu Lai since I came in–country.

Later in the day, after I got myself composed, I went back to headquarters looking for the first sergeant. The sergeant major had told me to get the bugle from the Top. All he could find was an old beat up thing with dents in it. Then it dawned on me. I said, "Wait a minute—man, my trumpet. My trumpet is inside of my chest locker back in Chu Lai." That was where I had to go anyway. It was all coming around. I thought, why, man, how ironic. There had to be a God. Who the heck told me to bring my trumpet, but God. Who told me I was going to need my trumpet? Why the hell did I bring a trumpet? I was going in the boonies. Did I know that I was going to end up being a bugler? No earthly way. I thought about that over and over again. Who on earth would have known? I didn't tell myself, packing my things that day before I got ready to go, that I was going to become a bugler and that was why I was going to need my trumpet. God just told me, "Put your trumpet in there."

In the meantime, I took their bugle back to my hootch and sat there on the edge of the bed with it in my hand. I could practice, anyway. Most of my days were spent practicing and waiting for orders to come through for Chu Lai. Nobody told me I had to do anything. I didn't even have to wash a dish. The only thing I did was eat, sleep, and play the bugle.

In the meantime, I wasn't making any friends. I didn't want to make any waves. I didn't want to start getting with the wrong guys, getting high, and then getting busted. I wanted to get high, but I thought I just better cool it; I didn't know these guys; I didn't know how careless they were. I mostly kept to myself for about two weeks.

Finally, after about two weeks, one of the guys in the mess hall invited me to come up to his hootch one night. He'd seen me around and we finally started talking. By this time I was polishing my boots. I was getting into the mentality of the rear. The guy said, "Hey, man, why don't you come up to the hootch, man. I got some dynamite smoke. Listen, man, we got a dyna-

mite hootch." At that time it was how much music, how much
entertainment could you put in your hootch? It was like coming
to somebody's house. These guys had two or three tape record-
ers. You could buy a tape recorder over there for seventy-five
dollars that would cost you three or four hundred dollars here.
Aretha Franklin and the Temptations were very, very popular with us at that time. Blacks were comparing her with the
Beatles. I used to hear Aretha Franklin sing and it would bring
tears to my eyes. I wanted to go to their hootch, but I also
wanted to avoid any problems. I thought, well man, I'd better
be cool; I didn't know these guys. They had a proper MOS, and
I didn't. If I fucked up, I was gone. No Article 15 for me. So I
didn't go. I started getting negatives from them because they
kept inviting me, and I never showed. "Where's this guy coming from? Who the hell does he think he is, a pet or something?"
    This was the first time I had even been put in a predicament
where I had to play white over black and black over white; I
had to operate. I had to play everybody. In my past dealings,
I hadn't had to contend with that. Being out of the South with
only two years in San Francisco, I was accustomed to black
with black, black over black. I had no white friends in San
Francisco. For me, all of a sudden, to learn that I had to be
friends with whites, blacks, anybody, was a very transitional
thing. Some guys get it when they go to integrated schools. They
begin to be social equals, dating whites, having white friends.
Me, I got it in the armed forces. So there I was, contending with
equality, which was driving me up the wall. I said to myself,
"Well, Stan, you just have to be strong and deal with it, that's
all there is to it." I was completely uncertain what was going to
happen. I wasn't even assigned to a unit. Their futures were
solid but they did not realize what my situation was. I'd been in
the boonies, I'd been shot at, seen guys get blown away, and
they hadn't. So a cold war was developing because I wouldn't
socialize with these guys, white or black. I lived with them, but
I didn't go to their hootch.
    One of these guys got smart with me in the mess hall. I didn't

like the piece of meat he put on my plate. He said, "What's wrong with that meat?" I said, "Hey, man, I just don't like it." Then I knew that they were getting upset. Trouble was coming. They didn't understand that being on that base was very strange to me. So I said to myself, "Oh shit, this is all I need." Then suddenly the spell was broken. The sergeant major sent down the orders for me to go to Chu Lai. That was what broke the cold war.

The next morning I was sitting down on the landing zone, ecstatic, really hyper, waiting for this Chinook to come in. When I saw that white sand of Chu Lai, I just started grinning from ear to ear. I found out what my company was, where my headquarters were, and I ran back there. The first thing I did was go inside of this hootch where my foot locker was. I told the clerk my name was Goff from Bravo Company, 196th Infantry Brigade, and I'd like to get my things out of my foot locker. I had to fill out this form. He says, "You going home?" I said, "No, I'm not going home, but I'm a brigade bugler." He goes, "You're a WHAT?" "I'm a brigade bugler." "You're kidding me. They got a bugler out there?" I say, "Yeah. Don't they have a bugler here?" He says, "Yeah, I guess they got a bugler here. I never hardly hear the God damn thing though. I'm always asleep." These guys back in Chu Lai were living the life of Riley. And I was just sort of getting onto the syndrome of what it was really like in the rear.

I filled out all these papers and got my personal belongings. And there was my trumpet. I started grinning from ear to ear. I picked it up and sort of petted it. I said, "Man, YOU are going to keep me out of the boonies."

The next thing to do was to find out how to get to division headquarters. I got instructions to ride a big truck back to the division along with some other guys that were going into town. Guys could tell I was from the boonies; I'm black and what the hell was I doing back here with all this spit and polish? But I got to see the first sergeant of division headquarters, and he gave me instructions on how to get to band headquarters. It so

happened that the bugler was there. So I introduced myself to
him. While we were talking, I was astounded to find out that
he actually didn't play any more. I said, "You're kidding?"
"No, I'm not kidding," he said, "it's nothing but a recording.
But, I recorded it." Then I cracked up. I said, "Oh, I see." He
had the tape. "Here are all the calls right here," he said. "The
sergeant major has been trying to get this tape, and every time
he comes in, he misses me or I miss him." He was so relaxed;
taking all this for granted. He said, "Here's the tape right here.
I don't know whether you've got a tape recorder back there or
not. Maybe you should listen to these things." So we listened
to it. I said, "There isn't a tape recorder at Baldy. I don't know
what he's going to do about that, anyway." "Well, maybe he
expects you to play it here and then you can maybe tape it, some
time he'll come home with a tape recorder." He never did. If I
had not listened to it, it would have been all ad lib.

I listened to the calls all that day and the next day. Then I
shook the guy's hand, thanked him very much for his cooperation, took the tape and went back to Baldy. The sergeant major
hadn't told me to stay up there three days. I didn't want to blow
it, staying up there endlessly. Get back on my own turf, know
where I am, and relax—that was my plan.

I went back out to LZ Baldy. Checked in with the Top. With
me being gone a couple of days, the guys in the mess hall sort of
forgot the cold war. Anyway, they sort of warmed up. I don't
know, maybe they heard something. When I got back, there
was no problem. Guys even said, "What's happening?" I was
really shocked, and thought, wow, it was great. Now that I
was back, I was going to go up and see them. And it was a good
idea, too, because then they found out—I was black as they
were. I was trying to cover my own ass like they were trying to
cover their ass. And after they found it out and had a chance to
talk about it, we really got tight. They were my buddies. By the
time I left Baldy, I knew every black guy in that headquarters
company, and they all knew me. It was really beautiful.

Stan

12 THE COLONEL'S MESS

After two and a half more weeks, Top came down one morning — I never will forget it — and he said, "You're going to be assigned to the colonel's mess. You'll be personally assigned to Colonel Kroesen's staff." I thought, the colonel's staff! Shit, I was at home with that. I'd been working in hotels as bus boy all my life. I packed my rucksack and I threw it on my back. The damn thing sure felt strange. I hadn't had a rucksack on for months and I was already dying with the weight — and it didn't have anything much in it.

I walked up to the colonel's mess, where I met Poncho, a Puerto Rican guy. I introduced myself, and he said, "Me, I'm Poncho." "What's happening, Poncho?"

"Oh, man, this is the life, the life, the life . . . " He was always like that, really a great guy. "Just having fun, man, fun . . ." "What are you getting ready to do?" "Oh shit, man, I got nothing to do until eleven o'clock." "Is that right?" "Yeah, man. Are you assigned up here or what, man? Are you gonna work up here? I see your rucksack and all, are you moving in

or what?" "Yeah, I guess I am." "You assigned up here?" I say,
"Yeah." "Oh, man, that's good. I really need some help."
I said, "What do you do?" "I'm a waiter, man. I'm a waiter.
Maybe you gonna be a waiter too. You a cook?" I said, "No, I
don't cook." "Then you gotta be a waiter." "I guess so, man."
"Aw, grab that bunk over there, it's empty." "OK, man."

A waiter, damn, I was feeling great. "Now, let me tell you,
man," he got serious. "Cut all the bullshit out. I like bullshit,
but I can be serious, too." He was a real smart guy; he knew
how to play the game, and he knew all kinds of games. "Now
listen," he said, "there's this head waiter, man. He don't like
brothers." Like that, right off the top. The head waiter's name
was Woody, and he was from Louisiana. He had more time in
the mess than anybody; that was why he was in charge of the
waiters. He turned out to be one of those flake white boys, sharp
but crooked. His trip was anything that could make him look
good and make you look bad. He had got hit in the arm by some
shrapnel and had grinned and lied his way out of the boonies.
This was the kind of white boy I'd heard about from Piper. So
that was all the more reason that I hated him.

While Poncho was hipping me to Woody, he came to the
door. Poncho immediately started getting back into his thing;
he was a real sharp guy: "Yeah, man, you gonna like it up here,
man. Hey, Woody come in, man." Woody says, "Yeah?" and
started grinning. "Come over here and meet our new waiter,
man. This is Stanley, man. Stanley, this is Woody." As soon as
I saw him, he gave me this big southern "good ole boy" grin.
I knew he was a bastard right off the bat. "How ya doin'?" He
didn't know me from beans, but he was grinning at me, shaking
my arm off. "How ya doin', Stanley?" "Oh, not too bad, man."
"You just get in?" I'm thinking to myself, "You motherfucker,
get out of my face." I didn't grin one iota; I just looked at him.
And I could tell he knew I wasn't buying his bullshit. Then his
tone turned serious. "You from the field, man?" I say, "Yeah."
"What you do to get up here, man?" He wanted to know that
right off the bat. "Shit, man, I didn't do anything. I'm just the

bugler." "Oh, I see—" He was shocked at that, too. "A
bugler?" "Yeah, I'm a bugler." "Oh, is that right? This is in
addition to your job assignment?" "Right." "I see. OK." Then
he said to Poncho, "Well, we're going to be going down in about
thirty minutes. I came up here to get you." So Poncho turned
around and said, "Man, you didn't come up here to get me. You
knew I was coming down there, anyway. What are you lying
about, Woody? You're starting out right off the bat giving the
man a bad impression of me. Now, you didn't have to come up
here to get a light bulb." They started bullshitting with each
other. Maybe he did or didn't come up to get him, but all three
of us walked back down to the mess.

Inside the mess I met Sergeant Williams, the black mess sergeant. At this time, no one here knew who the hell I was or why
I'd been sent to the rear. Nobody'd briefed them. So the sergeant
was quickly taken aback when he saw me walk through the
door. He was about to say, "What the hell you doing in here?"
I could see he was stiffening up, but Poncho said, "Hey, Sarge,
meet our new waiter." So the sergeant said, "Oh, I see, you're
the new waiter. Right. Oh. OK." You could see him sort of
laughing, thinking, God damn, they sent a black waiter . . . I
knew he was wondering right then what the shit did he do to get
up here? He said, "Well, now I got a white, I got a Puerto
Rican, and I got a black. That's all right." He started making
jokes about it. "We're going to keep this thing multi-racial,
there's no doubt about that." But I could tell, he was really
shocked. There were no black waiters in the colonel's mess,
never had been. I met the other guys in the mess. Besides
Williams, there was a black cook and a white cook. Jim was
black—a damn good cook; Fred couldn't cook worth a God
damn. He was a big fat dude, but he was all right. He was one
of those slow thinking guys, but once he had it, he had it. Sergeant Williams explained my duties to me. The other waiters
would show me exactly how to set up. Then I saw Vietnamese
back in the kitchen washing dishes. I said to Poncho, "Damn,
we don't have to pull KP, man?" And he said, "No, we're

waiters." I thought to myself, wow, this was really something. I didn't have to worry about washing the dishes.

By noon we were set up. About 12:15 p.m., the first couple of officers walked in. I heard their speech; they were from the South. I stiffened up immediately. I wasn't sure what these guys were going to say. Were they going to call me, "boy?" Every officer that came in was either a captain or a major or a light colonel. No lieutenants in the colonel's mess. So I was thinking, oh, Christ, every one of them was from the South. Nobody'd said anything to me quite yet. Then I saw one look up and say to another officer, "Hm, got a new waiter. Sending a nigger up; blah, blah, blah." Then they saw my name tag. "Oh, well, he earned his way up here."

The officers went through the same type of trip as the enlisted men, except that enlisted men stood in line getting their own plate loaded. In the officer's mess, the cooks in the back loaded the plates for the officers. It was great food, too. I couldn't wait to eat it myself. I remember that it wasn't overcooked or under-cooked—you could tell everything was fresh. Everyone in the mess hall was still talking, but the mumbling was getting to a minimum. I was wondering why, and I looked up and peered way over everybody. I thought, oh, this must be the command-ing officer. Beside him was another officer who turned out to be Lt. Colonel Milliner.

Colonel Milliner opened the door for the other officer. It's really strange how military rank works. These guys were all career military right down to the bone. Everything was done by seniority–rank; so the light colonel opened the door for the full colonel. Chairs scraped back and everybody jumped up. The waiters were supposed to stop immediately wherever we were. I saw the other waiters stop, and I stopped. Woody gave me an intimidating look. Hell, I'd already stopped. What the fuck was he looking at? I could tell right off the bat what Poncho told me was true. He just wanted to make sure that everyone knew that he was the sergeant waiter. The colonel walked to his seat, looked around, and then sat down; and as he sat down, every-body else sat down. Then everybody started talking again.

The colonel just sort of glanced at me. I learned later that Colonel Kroesen didn't treat everyone the same. If he respected you, then you were his man. He was really a powerful man, and I had a lot of respect for him. I found out later this man was one of the most intelligent colonels. I don't mean just in military tactics, but overall; he taught mathematics, I think, at West Point before coming to Vietnam. He was his own man. Always kept himself in shape, very lean. He always had a swagger to his walk. I studied that guy from day one because he was unique. That day he didn't look at me any particular way, just like I was another man, and I liked that.

After that first day of serving the colonel's mess, the work was pretty uneventful. The officers were always talking about the war, about strategy. I had one guy that called me boy one day. He said, "Boy, listen, what I want . . . " I just looked at him, and the captain next to him nudged him. I don't know what the captain said to him under his breath, but the colonel was looking right at him. I just left. I didn't know that the colonel was staring at him, but the captain must have told him, "Look, this guy is not a shammer." At that time it was a common practice for guys to sham to get in the mess hall. So most of the officers looked at them as shammers. The next day, man, I didn't have any problems at all in that mess hall. Nobody called me boy. They asked me what my name was. One southern guy said, "What's your name?" I said, "I'm Goff." He said, "OK, Goff, I need some more coffee." And afterwards, believe it or not, they always asked me, "please" and everybody called me Goff. There was no question the colonel had everything to do with that. I mean, how else? They would have been stomping on my behind to get me to break, because they were envious of the fact that I was up for the DSC. Well, the colonel stopped all that bullshit.

All the time that I was working in the colonel's mess, I was practicing the trumpet every day. One evening, the colonel announced to all the officers that we were going to have a bugler. I was just about to serve somebody's plate, and the colonel shouted out, "There's our bugler, right over there," and everybody looked around. I felt about two feet tall. I just started smiling, you know. "You're going to play that bugle for us, Goff, is that right?" "Yes sir, no doubt about it." So he said, "When are you going to start playing? I've been waiting on the sergeant major to tell me when this is going to start." He was smiling. I said, "Well, I'm waiting for the sergeant major to tell me that it's ready to go." He said, "Well, why don't we get it started?"

I guess I'd been in the rear about six weeks before they were actually ready for me to start. I don't know why it took so long, but that's the army for you, hurry up and wait. Another three weeks went by before I actually started playing. The sergeant major stopped me one day after the colonel mentioned it, and he told me he wanted me to start playing. He said, "Are you ready? I want to hear a wake-up call tomorrow morning at six o'clock."

I was standing on the hill, bright and early, at six o'clock on the dot the next morning. As a guy raised the flag up, I started playing the wake-up call — reveille. With the echo in the hills and me standing on a vantage point, they could hear me all over the LZ. Then I did a chow call at noon and a retreat in the evening at 5:30.

In addition to our other duties, some of us started building a bunker onto our tent. At that time, we had no bunker to run to in case of a rocket or mortar attack except the colonel's bunkers. So we were authorized to build a bunker. At first it was a lot of fun; then it got to be work. But I would always get out of it, because I had to go prepare for my calls or prepare the mess. The guys were filling sand bags all the time, and supposedly they had recruited some other guys to help fill them. The colonel's drivers were in the tent right next door, with the mess people. He only had two drivers. They had been wounded. Everybody had some sham, but you couldn't say that these guys hadn't paid their dues. They'd all been hit; even Woody had gotten hit. No one could say that these guys were goldbricking; they were there as part of a deliberate choice by the colonel.

One day, I was just sitting there living the life of Riley, and I looked up, and there was Carl, my buddy from out in the boonies. Carl told me he came in out of the boonies because he was ill; he said he'd almost cracked up out there, and they sent him in for a few days' rest and to see a doctor. Carl had been in the boonies steadily something like seven or eight months. I'd been in the rear about three months. Carl had been in-country maybe a month longer than I had. He had about four months to go. He'd heard that I was up here, and he wanted to come up and see where I was. "Ah, man," he said, "you're living the life up here, man." I said, "Yes, it's not too bad . . ." He said, "Wow, man, I'd give my eye tooth to be back here." I said, "I understand man, I do, no doubt about it." We sort of talked on a down-to-earth basis. At first, I didn't notice how uptight he was. He seemed like he was fine, except that I could tell he was tired. I could see the weakness in his body. I took him back to the bunker. (By this time we had it completed.) I took him around and Sergeant Smith met him. I asked the sergeant, "Could he stay here for a while with us?" He wanted to stay up there with me. Sergeant Smith said, "Yeah, long as he doesn't overdo it, try to take advantage of it." Sergeant Smith had had some experience with that before. So he said, "Yeah, he can stay with you. Should be an extra cot there." So the cat crashed up there with me. Later Sergeant Smith said, "Now, this guy's not AWOL, is he?" I said, "No, he's not AWOL." I brought back food for him from the mess. After Carl had stayed there a day or so, Sarge started telling me, "Your buddy doesn't seem too right, Stan. Are you sure he's OK?" I sort of played it off. But I could tell, Carl would get off on a track and keep going. He wasn't sharp like he used to be. He was reminiscing all the time, and he wasn't ever thinking about the future. I noticed that he never talked about going back to his unit. He was just partying with us all night—which was fine. Poncho and I even carried him up on the hill with us one night. We had a great time. I thought the guy was just strained. Later Sarge said, "Shouldn't he be checking back with his unit? He stays up there all day.

I never see him going to the doctor or anything. I thought he was sent in to see a doctor and he was supposed to report back out."

About the third day Smith was really getting on my back about Carl. The sergeant said he smelled because he hadn't taken a bath. He'd been up there three days without a change of clothes. He said, "Where's his clothes? Listen, Stan, I believe this man is AWOL. Now, I don't want to have to call the field marshal." The provost marshal was in charge of the military police on the post. He said, "I don't want to have to tell Major Williams about this guy. I want you to tell him yourself, Stan, all right? He's your buddy and he comes from your unit. I understand you fought side by side, so I want you to tell him that he's going to have to leave." I said "All right, Sergeant Smith, I'll do it."

When I went back up there to tell Carl, he really pounced all over me. He had seemed fine until I told him that he was going to have to go back. I said, "Where is our unit right now?" "Oh, man, you don't give a God damn . . . " That was when he went sort of berserk. He called me everything except a child of God; he cursed me out, told me I was an Uncle Tom, all kinds of bullshit. I said, "Man, I'm sorry, Carl. I've been told you can't stay here any more. I would love to have you stay, man." "Oh, you lying motherfucker, you just looking after your own God damn self; you don't give a shit." I said, "Man, I understand, I'm awfully sorry, man, really I am. I hate that I have to tell you that, man." He said, "I wish you could think of anything." I said, "I can't think of anything to enable you to stay on, man." He just claimed that I wasn't trying to help him out at all. I'd had him stay up there three or four days; he didn't have to do anything except sit there and rest. I had him right up there, man, but he told me that I didn't try to help him. Obviously, he wasn't himself—the man was tired, and I could understand. I would have been the same way, probably.

I watched Carl go on down the street, and that was the very last time I saw him. He brought the reality of the boonies back

to me for the first time in months. Of course, the whole episode
kept going through my mind. That night after work I said, "The
hell with it. I know I tried to do everything I possibly could to
make the guy feel at home." Poncho told me, "Hey man, don't
take that personally; you know the guy's sort of—off, man."
All the guys told me that. I said, "Oh, I know it." I had a good
drunk and forgot all about it.

Bob

13 WOUNDED

We were working in and out between the mountains and the valleys and down by Phan Rang on the coast, humping back and forth, wherever some action would ignite. We'd jump on choppers and go in on a combat assault. We were always on the go. We'd work an area for fifteen or twenty days through the swamps or hills and, if we didn't make any contact, we'd hear that somebody had been hit and here were the choppers to pick us up. That was the nature of airborne as a striking force. We moved around quite a bit, which is why I got the Air Medal; you have to have at least twenty–five combat assaults out of a chopper after six months in hostile territory. We was always where the heat was. We took documents off the enemy dead that, when they were translated, said to avoid the 173rd by all means. They called us "the herd" when we were in Vietnam, because they thought we were animals. We were unshaven, nasty, dirty, and stinking. Our attitude was piss poor; everyday we had a case of the ass. So when we made contact, it wouldn't take us too long to break contact. We'd bring so much scunnions, it would make Charlie move on out. He was losing a lot dealing with us. Everywhere we went we'd quiet the area down. It really didn't matter what company of the 173rd it was. All those hard times and stuff pushed us to the point where we were just like machines. We were tough, and we knew how to function under extreme pressure with total unity and harmony. We felt that no one could beat us. In fact, that was our motto: "First in the Nam, second to none." We didn't want to be there, though; I didn't. But I said to myself, "Since I am here, since I don't want to die, I'm going to do my best to saturate the area with fire — just so I *can* live."

I walked point with the M-79. There were usually four 79s in the company, one per platoon. The M-79 man could walk just about anywhere. If there were a couple of extra 79s, which we had sometimes, depending on the area we were in, they would be mid-way in the platoons. There really was no standard operating procedure. I thought the M-79 was a good point weapon. Actually, I felt better with that than I did with the M-16. Of course, you'd never walk point with the pig. Your firepower would be too vulnerable. But I would walk third from the point man with the pig sometimes. When we went on eight or nine-man patrols, I used to walk right in back of the compass man. In case we got hit, I was right there to lay out some smoke.

We kept tramping through the jungle going nowhere. It seemed like we was going in circles.

My pig was being humped by this brother from Little Rock, Arkansas, named Lee. When I got back from R & R, I heard that the company commander had warned him about the weapon. He checked the gun while I was gone and found out that Lee hadn't cleaned it for five or six days. The monsoon was just about over, but the rain had started to rust inside the barrel and all up inside the chamber. The CO had made Lee clean it up right there in front of him. At first, he was gonna take the gun away from him. Instead, when I got back to the field, he told me to keep a close eye on Lee. I was supposed to make sure that he'd keep proper maintenance on the gun. So I didn't take the pig back; I just made sure that he'd clean the gun so it would be ready for firing. That was why I was assigned to my old platoon when I got back to the field. The company commander put me in the gun squad as assistant gunner even though I was humping the M-79. In case something happened and the gunner couldn't operate, the assistant took over. Before I left the field, Lee had been my ammo bearer. So the company commander kept me near the pig, which pissed me off.

Later we moved into a hilly area toward Dalat. I was walking point with the 79, going up a hill, with the gunner not far away. Another brother named William Patton carried the compass right in back of me. As Lee was humping the pig, he fell out. The hill was so steep that he got fatigued. For a while he tried to make it, but eventually he just completely collapsed. So I reacquired the pig. Actually, I just got pissed and took it. I didn't like the way the company commander was talking to Lee, and I didn't like the way Lee seemed to be bullshitting. The CO was talking to him rough, "Get your God damn ass up, you no good asshole. You gonna pretend you can't be a man up here? Everybody else is keeping up, why don't you keep up?" I had mixed feelings about the situation. I could see that the company commander was right, in a way, but I didn't think he should be pushing Lee. I thought he was bullshitting at first myself, but then I could see clearly that he was badly fatigued. Everybody was exhausted. I was, too, after living the good life on R & R. Some of those hills were drastic, you'd reach out for branches and little trees; you needed all the help you could get.

Most of the guys didn't think it was Lee's fault. We knew that he humped the gun good on flat ground. He wasn't used to humping it in the hills. That extra twenty-four pounds with all the extra ammo criss-crossed around your shoulders took getting used to. Lee wasn't used to carrying that weight. Hell, it took several months to get used to carrying the pig. So he wasn't really half-stepping. He was a very skinny guy, so he was just out of it. Everybody was feeling sorry for him, trying to help him up. Some of the guys were even taking some of his canteens to hump for him until we got off the slope. So that was how I reacquired that motherfucking pig. Then, when we got to the top of the mountain, a big fire fight broke out. I had the pig on one flank and Bobby Taylor had the other pig on the opposite flank. From that point on, I kept the pig until I got hit.

We'd been moving into this mountainous area toward Dalat. That was where we ran into this big NVA base camp and got hit. As we tried to take this one hill the first line got wiped out. The company commander yelled for everyone to move forward, "Move on the flanks, cover the flanks!" When we tried to move forward, they dusted us. A lieutenant must have been hit with a B-40 rocket cause it just ripped him up; the whole upper part of his body was cut off. About four other people with him got killed at the top of the mountain in that first exchange. And it wouldn't let up.

That was when we knew we were in a heavy fire fight against a major unit. They started hitting us from the front and from the flank. We started moving, though: "Come on, move up, move up, get the guns up here." That was what the company commander was yelling. "Get them guns up here," talking about the machine guns. He wanted the pigs on the point. It seemed like there wasn't any way in the world we could do it, but we got my gun up. At this point, our pigs wouldn't do any good because those mothers up the hill had a couple of 50s. They were knocking down trees with that shit and firing rockets, too. Plus they tried to surround us on the flank to try to choke us off. So the CO got on the horn. We had to back them up, now. If we didn't hold them back at this point, they'd just overrun us. They could have if they wanted to, I guess. They had the high ground. So we started climbing this hill, trying to get at them. Shit was flying everywhere, and we didn't know if Charlie would flank us; seemed like we was in a big L-shaped ambush. That was how the shit was hitting—from straight in front and above and from the right on our flank.

We tried to take that hill for about two hours and couldn't do any good. Those mothers had us backing up, they were throwing so much scunnions out at us. The company commander had been on the horn, but it seemed we had walked clean out of artillery range. So they had us. Then he asked for air support, calling in our big brothers, you know. Every grunt loved the Phantoms. Pretty soon, they came swooping in dropping napalm. They broke the strangle hold on us; Charlie broke contact.

It turned out Charlie was in fortified bunkers in the biggest base camp I'd ever seen. They had something like three or four hundred bunkers. It was strange, the way they had it. They picked the ridgeline as the perfect spot. All around the ridge, on each side, there was nothing but fortified bunkers. But that made it easier for the Phantoms to hit them. The place was like a home base that they had been operating out of for maybe six months or so. They had places set up where they had been barbecuing pigs.

After the fighting was over, I looked down. My leg was bloody, the blood just draining out of my boot. I had been so scared and fighting so hard, I didn't know I was hit. Plus, I'd burned up two barrels on the pig I was using. I'd really melted down the first one and by the time the shit broke off, the second one was about to go. We lost about eight or nine dead and about twenty wounded. We picked up about thirty NVA and they all had AKs. You couldn't bring them out of the country. The NVA was running the banana clips with the bayonet tucked underneath. I checked it out. The AK is a pretty sharp weapon. It fires a little faster than the M–16, so they jam after a fire fight. We'd just go around picking them up. We found different kinds of stuff we had to turn in; rain gear in the bunkers, bags of rice, everything they left behind when they ran away. We found blood trails everywhere, too. They were dragging their dead and wounded away as they moved out. I guess they knew that when the Phantoms dropped the napalm that was the end of the

battle. They dashed off down the mountain. I used to look at
that napalm and say to myself, "I'm glad I'm on your side,
brother."

For the next few days our guys stayed out there and cleaned
up the area. Then the whole unit moved back to the rear. But
I went out with the dustoffs. They ran the casualties to different hospitals at Tuy Hoa and Nha Trang. At first they were
going to send me to Okinawa because I was short—I got
wounded a couple of months before I was to come home. Then
they changed their minds and sent me to Tuy Hoa. I had got hit
low down on the shinbone; the slug just fractured it. It didn't go
straight in, nothing like that. I didn't get medivacked right
away because the fighting was pretty intense when I got hit.
They didn't want to take any chance of bringing in choppers
right away.

After the fighting, the dustoffs came in and took us to the aid
station in the rear, located right at the fire support base that
my unit was operating out of. The doctors and medics there
did what they could for me—stopped the bleeding and kept the
wound from getting infected. At first, when I got hit, I didn't
feel anything. I was too scared and I was concentrating on
Charlie. I felt a little stinging, but I didn't think nothing of it.
If I'd been hit in the neck or my arm was coming off, that would
have been different. At the same time, I'd still have been trying
to fight; I didn't want to die over there. That was one thing I
didn't want to do!

In three or four hours, the choppers came back in to evacuate
us to the 8th Field Hospital at Nha Trang. I saw dudes coming
in that were really hurt. That was why I didn't feel so bad. I had
what they called a surface wound. I was looking at these other
guys, and I was thinking, man, oh man, these dudes . . . One
of them lost a leg, another an arm. I really felt shitty, not about
my wound, but about those cats. I knew they'd just be out of it
and I resented the fact that we were in Vietnam more than ever
now. I realized that I could be lying there much worse than I
was. There were guys trying to console other guys being brought

in, but I knew, if a guy had a limb gone, how could he be consoled? I was thinking, he was going to be like that for the rest of his life, no matter which way the war came out. He was going to be missing a limb, man. Shit!

They knew I had been in the field. Everybody knew everybody. And these guys were very resentful. Some wanted to die; you could see it in their faces. Some were screaming and cursing as they were being taken down corridors in the hospital.

GIs don't benefit from wars. I felt like most of the troops in Vietnam. We felt that we were just as patriotic as anybody, but we were in the wrong situation. Today, everybody's forgotten about those cats. Even today it's on my mind. How are they surviving? It seems like when we came back to the World, nobody seemed to care. I felt I could understand the hatred I could see in their eyes. I know how I felt. If they'd have had to amputate my leg or whatever, I think I would have just taken a hand grenade and blown myself away. I wasn't coming back like that.

The guys used to talk about that in the field: "If I lose a leg, don't let 'em send me out. If I lose consciousness, and if you can do it without being seen, blow me away." We meant it. I told my partners, "If I lose a leg or arm or something like that, blow me away, man, if you can do it without somebody seeing you. I don't want you to go to jail for murder." It wouldn't have been murder to me; it would have been a favor. But, of course, common sense tells you the army would have made it murder. I never wanted them to send me back to the states as a cripple.

The hospital was full of guys that were hurting. Hopping around that hospital, man, I saw just about everything. In fact, being nosy like I am, I used to go in places you weren't supposed to go. Nurses actually chased me away. I saw guys with no privates, no penis. I saw guys with no legs, with one leg, one arm. Once they destroyed some part of your body, then it takes a lot just to go on. Guys do it, though!

I was at the 8th Field Hospital at Nha Trang for twenty–nine days. The hospital was right down the beach from the town of

Nha Trang. You could catch those little Lambrettas and go up
to the town. The post at Nha Trang was serviced by hundreds
and hundreds of Vietnamese workers out of Nha Trang and surrounding villages. They had a little bus stop there where the
Lambrettas would line up like taxis. It was the Vietnamese
transportation system — for the ones that didn't have bicycles.
The women especially came into Camp McDermott to do cooking and cafeteria work, laundry for the troops, any type of little
job. Camp McDermott was a big place. Vietnamese women
would be working in the hospital, along with the GIs, of course.
The hospital area itself was like a city. So the Lambrettas
would haul people constantly back and forth between the post
and the town.

Along the beach between Nha Trang and 8th Field Hospital,
some of the officers had large houses that they rented from the
Vietnamese. They were staying off the post. Right there in front
of all this they had a resort area running about five miles —
nothing but white sandy beach with all these dudes out there
suntanning. They had security all around the city of Nha
Trang. It was like an in-country R & R center; they could lay
out there without a weapon or anything. Everyone would kinda
kick back. I would put on an old straw hat, stoop over so I
wouldn't be noticeable; whoever seen a Vietnamese 5 feet 10½
inches? So I would slip out of the compound, get a Lambretta,
give papa-san fifty P and I'd be downtown.

Sometimes MPs would stop you and say they was looking for
a guy with such and such a patch. If he was in town loafing
and loitering, they would try to find him and bring him back to
the compound and turn him in to his unit. They would patrol
constantly with jeeps. A lot of guys were shamming, man.
You'd go into a bar and it would be full of GIs from all units,
kicking back, drinking beer, bullshitting, smoking dope. When
the MPs would come, they'd scatter. Some guys would have
those excuse-type papers to be in town. You could get Ameri-
can-type food, almost any type of beer you wanted. That stuff
was coming right off the base. I said, "Hey, what is this?" I had

some really funky feelings about what I saw, because all the time I'd been in the field, I thought everybody in the Nam was fighting. I'd never seen a town this big since I'd been to the Nam. I'd never seen GIs lounge around, and all the time I was thinking back to my partners in the boonies. I was thinking, hey, they didn't even know this was happening. Like I never knew until I saw it.

You had your choice of women, choice of food. They had something like a discotheque up there where you could get cold beer and nice girls. You had everything you needed. At the restaurant, they had tables and they'd put a napkin down in front of you—it was like I was back in the states for a minute. It boggled my mind to the point where I was thinking there was a lot of corruption going on there, a lot of bullshit going on. And they got us out there in the field going through all this hell and here were all these guys sitting on their ass having a vacation. And they were getting hazardous duty pay just like the guys in the field.

What blew my mind was that it was so much like stateside. In Nha Trang I saw starched and ironed fatigues, shined jump boots, and I was nasty and dirty. When I got back from the field, I didn't have any clothes, so I went to a supply clerk and got him to give me some. That was what made it easy for me to get in and out of the compound; they couldn't determine which unit I was in. You had to have ID on you; hospital papers, unit patch, or a letter from your liaison officer. I had my hospital papers, but I wasn't supposed to be in town; that was why I had to slip out. When I discovered that they didn't have a roster and weren't going to call my name, I just stayed in town.

I met a girl there. She worked in the cafeteria. I used to talk to her in the cafeteria, and later she invited me into town. We got kinda close, just from talking. She knew my situation; knew I was horny from the woods. She insisted that I stay up at her place in Nha Trang during the day. She'd bring food from the cafeteria. She knew when the MPs came through, what I should do if they knocked on the door. She lived alone. Her husband

and her daughter had gotten killed around Saigon years ago. Her father had died in the French war. She spoke English fluently. I would stay down with her for two or three days at a time before coming back to the base. And she would tell me, "Viet Cong right next door!" I had no weapon, no nothing. Hell, Charlie was there on his R & R. Anyway, she would take care of me. I hated to leave her, often I think back on her, wonder how she's doing. I wonder if she got killed when the Vietnamese made that last assault to take over the whole country.

Coming home was the best part of the war. Man, I can't even describe it. It was like being born again. I know one thing. This joker was double happy. In fact, when I landed at McCord Air Force Base, Washington, I got down and kissed the ground! They held us there for a couple of days for in-processing. The only thing I wanted to do was get out. I had quite a few medals. They dressed us up in our greens. But I threw all that shit away. I came home in a suit, and the only ribbon I wore home was the National Defense Ribbon—the first one they gave me after three or four months. I felt I had defended something. But at the time I was quite confused. I don't know what the fuck I had defended.

Stan

14 R & R IN HONG KONG

A really tremendous thing happened to me in January of 1969. I was getting an R & R. I had more money then than ever before in my life, about five hundred dollars, cold cash. I was very excited and packed up my little items ready to go. At the R & R center at Cam Ranh, they had all these countries where you could go. A sergeant came and told us about these countries, giving us the whole breakdown, the cultures, everything. He told us about veneral disease; that was the big thing. "Now, we gotta talk about VD. I know you guys have been without women. I know the first thing you're going to do— those of you that go that way. Only deal with the girls that have a medical card."

All my life I'd seen movies with Clark Gable and Vivien Leigh about Hong Kong. So I said, "Well, I'm going to go there."

I never will forget approaching Hong Kong. Suddenly I saw a huge cliff emerging from the ocean, like a city sitting on the edge of an island. The water was beating up the edge of this rock cliff. And then all of a sudden, we were landing. I don't know how the pilot actually landed; I never did see a strip, myself. We were there. Wow! I was getting off and my head was about twenty feet high.

I heard the guys talking about what they were going to do, but I didn't make any friends on that flight. We got on a bus and they took us to a large auditorium that was part of the city municipal center. They told us *again* about VD and gave us the names of good hotels. So it was not a bad orientation. They were doing it to help us, because they told us, "Once you're out there, you're on your own. If you get your heads knocked in, killed, anything . . . " Then he finally said, "Okay, now, we'll turn you loose." When he said that, boy, chairs rolled over, guys climbed all over themselves.

I hailed a taxi. I told this guy the name of the hotel that the instructor had recommended. It was a moderate hotel, not very expensive, but very, very clean, a very stately type of building. I admired the Chinese for the quality of their workmanship. I looked at the table, the hard wood floors—everything was handmade.

After a bath and some tea, I was back out on the street and saw this place called the Old Savoy Club. I got to Hong Kong thinking about Clark Gable and Vivien Leigh. Now I thought, wow, Billie Holiday used to sing at a club called the Old Savoy. So I walked in. Upstairs they had a lot of entertainment; downstairs at the bar was where the girls were. So I went downstairs. I was sitting there, having a drink, when mama–san approached me, "Hi, GI. You want a girl, GI? You want a girl?" I said, "Yeah, that's a good possibility." She say, "Oh, I got a girl for you, GI." She showed me one girl. She was a little skinny; I thought, not enough chest on her. Then she showed me another girl whom I didn't like at all. Then there was only one that wouldn't come or smile at me either. But she was really fine. I looked at her, and she looked at me, and then she started to take her hair down. Mama–san fussed at her in Chinese. Finally, this girl reluctantly came over.

But I said, "Naw, that's OK," and she went back. I knew

she was reluctant. Then I thought, what the hell, I liked her, and told mama-san she was the one. "You want *her?*" "Yeah, I want her. What's her name?" "Suzanne."

When Suzanne appeared after about five minutes, I began asking her, "What have you heard about black GIs? It's obvious you have heard something about black GIs that is causing you not to want to meet me." She said, "Oh, no, you got me all wrong. I like everybody. I'm not prejudiced." And immediately when she said that, I knew. They weren't familiar with that word; somebody had crowded that idea into her mind.

"Oh, you buy me a drink?"

So she got off the subject. I bought her a drink and we started talking. She said, "You like music?" I said, "I love music." She went over to the juke box and played a song by Esther Phillips —her first big hit, a love ballad. That became our theme song. We always played it, she and I.

We got to drinking. I knew nothing was in her drink, but as we drank I became more loose and canny, too; I wanted to collect my thoughts and not be anxious to let my physical desires overrule my good sense.

She said, "I'm very expensive, Stan. Can you afford me?" "Aw, come on, what do you mean, you're expensive? What are we talking about?" She said, "Oh, well—you interested?" "Sure I'm interested. Do you think I'd have you over here, talking with you? I could be down the street." She said, "OK. I go with you and we talk price in your room. You have to pay mama-san money to take me out." So I paid her five bucks just to get Suzanne out of the place.

I took her on back to my place and saw how really beautiful she was. Then I thought, wait a minute, don't get carried away and blow everything—I was getting to be a gullible mess here. She sat over on one side of the room, which pleased me. I sat back on the other side, watching her crossing and uncrossing her legs, letting me see what I wanted. We started talking about price. After a lot of dickering, we agreed on thirty dollars a night for the whole week.

It was a gentle love-making though it was all night long, very

gentle, because I really took it very slow with her. I wanted it
to be slow, because I wanted it to be good, to myself, as well
as to her. It was a great experience. I'd heard all kinds of stories
about prostitutes myself — that they had no feeling and stuff like
that, and that was all bullshit.

The next morning she awoke about nine o'clock. She awoke
with a start, like she didn't mean to really stay that long. She
said, "Oh, nine o'clock? I've got to get home." She said, "Oh,
Stan," but I knew she liked me, when she talked to me like that,
and even when she stayed that long and forgot herself as
Suzanne, professional prostitute, and became Suzanne, the
woman. She was only about twenty, my age. I was very impressed with her.

When she was ready to go, she said, "You're a real nice guy,
Stan." I said, "Well, will I be able to see you tonight?" "I don't
know, Stan; you don't pay me enough money, I need more
money. Tonight you talked me out of what I need to get. But
you're a real nice guy. If you want me, you come down there.
Then I know you want me." She was serious about that, looked
at me hard as she left. I thought, wow, I had to come all the way
to Hong Kong to fall in love! She was getting to me, just that
quick. I didn't want any other woman then. She had spoiled me.

So I crashed, and couldn't even fall asleep. Seven o'clock,
I couldn't hardly wait. I knew I didn't want to go there too
early, so I made myself stay away until about seven-thirty or
eight o'clock. But when I got near the Old Savoy, I almost ran
to that place, I was so anxious. As I got downstairs mama-san
came over and said, "Hi, GI, I heard. Suzanne called me. She
likes you." I said, "Really?" I'd gone all to pieces now, waiting
and waiting. She said, "I don't know where Suzanne is." I
thought maybe she hadn't showed up for work or something.
Finally about 9:30 p.m., like magic, I looked up and there
she was, smiling just so beautifully: "Where have you been?"
"Oh, I've been out — I hear you're looking for me." She got in
the booth and sat right beside me and squeezed my hand.

Suzanne and I decided to party that night. I wanted her to

show me Kowloon before going to my place. First she took me into plush night clubs where all the English were. There was a singer up there singing Dinah Shore–like tunes, sort of boring. We ate dinner and drank a little wine. She said, "You don't like, huh?" I said, "Oh, no, it's OK." She said, "No, you don't like. I take you to other club where there is a band." But this place really didn't have a lot of blacks either. I thought I would see other black GIs. Then she said, "I know. I know where to take you, Stan."

We went to a disco where I saw nothing but dark–skinned Chinese girls, and it blew my mind. My mouth fell open. I had never seen any dark–skinned Chinese girls. They were really getting down. I saw other black GIs. "Hey, what's happening, man? What's going on?" I was really coming loose. "Why didn't you take me here first?" She was giddy with laughter now, "Oh, I just wanted to save the best for last." But I thought to myself that she wasn't comfortable here. She was used to going to the other places. But she sat there. That was when I knew Suzanne liked me. She was so light–skinned, not white, but her skin was very pale. I could see the other girls were cutting her down. It was like they knew her or something. They were just staring at her, hard. I was having a good time, but she said, "We go, huh?" I started to say, "What do you mean? We just got here." We had only been there for an hour, and things were really getting bopping. I smelled a little smoke, and I thought maybe I might be able to angle around here, but since she was talking about going, we left. She really made love to me that night.

The next morning she asked about more money. She said, "Listen, Stan, I guess you know I've agreed to go ahead and stay with you all week. Yeah, I stay with you, Stan. I don't like the money that you're paying me. Why don't you pay me more?" I said, "No, Suzanne. There's no way I will do that. I'll pay you what we agreed every day, or at the end." She said, "OK, you pay me every day."

The next morning after I paid her, she said, "Maybe you want

to be alone one night; maybe you want to go out and see some
things on your own." I was sort of tired out. She was telling me
she had something else to do.

I went out and started walking down the street again, looking
at jade and jewelry. I passed some clubs and heard this soul
music, saw a lot of cuties, but wasn't interested. I couldn't
bring myself to pick out another woman. I stayed out to about
eleven o'clock and suddenly remembered, Suzanne was supposed to call me.

I got back to my room and waited until the phone rang.
"Stan, I'm coming over; you want to see me tonight?" "Sure, I
want to see you. You know that." She stayed with me all the rest
of the time, and I was very sad about leaving her. I even thought
about going AWOL.

When I returned to the Nam we wrote each other for a full
three months. Each time I'd write her, she'd write me back,
telling me things going on in Hong Kong. Finally, I saw the
opportunity for a leave. I had a good rapport with the officers,
especially Major Williams. I told him I would like to have
another leave.

When I got back to Hong Kong, I picked up the phone and
called the Old Savoy. Before I even hung up the phone, I was
down in the lobby, waiting. She came running down the side-
walk right into my arms. I just picked her up. "Oh, Stan, I'm
so happy to see you here, I'm just so happy!" I was happy, too.
Tears were in my eyes. She really didn't believe I was coming.
She said, "You told me you were coming, I just didn't believe
it."

The second time I left, it was a tear jerker. We were both
crying. She said, "I'll never see you again, I know, I know . . ."
I said, 'I'll write you. I'll write you and I'll send for you. But I
want you to make sure that it's a decision you really want. Once
you're in the states it's hard as shit to get back." She said, "I
know. I want to go. I want to go." I wrote her several letters
later at the Old Savoy, but never got a response. I said to myself, "Well, I guess you can hang it up, Stan." But when I got

back home, sure as shooting, a big package was waiting for me at the post office, all the way from Hong Kong. It had five suits in it, half-a-dozen shirts, another half-a-dozen ties. She sent that to me, but there the story of Suzanne ended.

Stan

15 THE MEDAL

After I got back from R & R, they were working on me getting the DSC. I didn't hear anything at all until Captain Milpas, my old company commander, came up to eat one day. He came to the door of the mess hall and I rushed out to shake his hand. He said, "I want to talk to you after dinner." He and Colonel Kroesen were coming to see General Geddes. After General Geddes had come and gone, Captain Milpas came back out there and started talking. "Listen, Goff," he said, "what I wanted to tell you is that we're having sort of a problem. General Geddes wants to knock your citation down to a Silver Star. He already has given Hardcore a Silver Star. But the colonel refuses to award you a Silver Star. The colonel is very disappointed, and I am, too. So the only thing I can tell you right now, Goff, is that that's why it's been held up so long. That's why you have not heard anything. But don't worry, as far as I'm concerned, you earned a DSC, and you are going to get a DSC. The colonel is in my corner. That's all I can tell you right now—OK, soldier?" I said, "OK, Captain Milpas, I understand —thank you very much."

I remember we had a change of Top—headquarters first
sergeant changed. This new Top knew about the DSC. We
started talking late one afternoon, about sunset. I had just
finished blowing the bugle and he was telling me that I sounded
good. Then he said, "You know what the DSC can do for you,
soldier?"

I said, "No. Not really."

"Well, listen," he said, "if you wanted a career in the military, you should take it right now. You wouldn't have any
problems at all. You'd probably be the youngest first sergeant
ever. You could retire with a full pension; you can get an extra
pension aside from your military pension." I said, "Really?"

"Sure, twenty years in the service, you get an extra pension
for the rest of your life just for having the DSC. In addition to
that, any kind of war at all that comes along, you never have
to go back." "Are you kidding?"

He said, "Nope. You can volunteer. They can draft you. But
they can't send you into combat."

Well, I thought that was quite significant—obviously.
"That's the first time anyone had ever told me about any
advantage in actually being the recipient of that type of an
award."

One day I was in the mess hall bullshitting with Sergeant
Smith and Jim, with my feet docked up on the table, doing
nothing, when the colonel came spinning back through there.
He looked at the sergeant, looked at Jim, and waltzed up to me,
and said, "Goff, congratulations. How does it feel to be a DSC
recipient?" Just like that. I thought to myself, oh, wow. I said,
"I can't believe it, Sir." He said, "Yes, you got it. I just came
back from Saigon, and General Abrams is going to give you the
award personally." My mouth just fell open. Sergeant Smith
and Jim heard it, too, and they were just all smiling from ear
to ear, proud of what was happening to me. After that, I
couldn't thank him enough. Everyone in the kitchen just about
melted into their chairs.

I had to wait another eight weeks for General Abrams to

show up. I was getting apprehensive as hell. On the day of the award, I started seeing men gathering all around, right in front of the new brigade headquarters. Finally, this captain came in and said, "OK, Goff, we're ready to go. You can come out now." As I walked with him, I felt like I was going to the gas chamber. He was saying, "Relax, man, relax. You're not going to a funeral. You're supposed to be happy today." I said, "Well, I am, you know. No problem, Sir." So we walked out on the steps, and I saw all these heads turn to look at me. By now, there were two to three hundred men out there. They brought a unit in from the field; not my company, but my unit was rep- resented—the 196th Infantry Brigade. I didn't get a chance to talk to these guys, but I saw them out of the corner of my eye. Captain Milpas was there. I remember Sergeant Needham; I saw Hardcore Castile. They let them get up close.

Guys were still gathering. The Captain positioned me, and then I saw the brigade sergeant major, now the division ser- geant major, and he inspected me. I thought to myself, "God damn, I hope it's all right." Then I saw a little smile come on his face and I thought I must have looked all right. In the end, he walked over to me and said, "Goff, you look great." He had given me his seal of approval. This was all an astounding exper- ience to me; I was speechless.

I heard the chopper coming. That was what we were all standing out there for—waiting for General Abrams, and I thought, GENERAL ABRAMS. There he was! The chopper landed, and he got off with his entourage of generals. General Abrams was a four-star general. He had several other generals with him and a Marine lieutenant general and many other officers.

I was standing there waiting and finally, out of the corner of my eye, I saw officers stiffening up. Finally, Colonel Kroesen walked out to greet Abrams. They had a small formal exchange and Kroesen saluted them. Then he turned around and started walking toward me. Abrams was looking at me and asking questions of the colonel. As I stood there, he came fully into view. He looked at me as he walked up. As he got closer, my heart went "BOOM." I was ready for him to say, "What's wrong with this guy? He doesn't even smile or nothing." I was trying to maintain my control. I saw a slight smile come across his face. Then I sort of acknowledged that smile, but I didn't break into a big grin. I thought to myself, "Now, don't blow it by grinning." I'm thinking black, too. "Don't blow it," grinning from ear to ear, Oh, yassuh, General, kind of bullshit. He had very steel, cold blue eyes, and they were very much in control. He didn't seem to be under any pressure, having to hurry up and get this out of the way. His movements were decisive. He looked at the medal, he looked at me. He held it up and pinned it on me. Then he looked at me, and said, "Congratulations, soldier." I said, "Thank you very much, Sir." "You're very welcome." Then he turned and made a quick right face. He went over and the colonel led him inside of a B–TOC.

After General Abrams disappeared into B–TOC, all the officers filed by me, and all of them shook my hand. It was all precision. It didn't seem like they had rehearsed it or anything. These guys were really pros; they didn't bullshit. I shook hands with every officer there, about eighty of them, including the generals down to the lowest lieutenant. The sergeant major of course came at the end. He said, "Goff, good job. Good job." And I knew I had done a good job for him, you know, in accepting the damn thing. It was quite an experience. It was an experience that obviously I'd never had in my life, but — it was something, it really was. After I shook all these guys' hands I was really tired.

Finally, some of my guys came up. Needham had been promoted. He and the other platoon sergeant shook my hand, "Congratulations, Goff." All officers were inside B–TOC now, and slowly all the guys were dispersing. I went back into Major Williams' headquarters and pulled off my utility belt, and then sort of eased off to my own quarters. I just sat on the bunk for a long time in shock. Every time I started thinking, did it really happen? I looked down and said, "Well, there's your proof." I just wanted to leave it there, you know. But I finally took it off. Most of the guys left me alone. They knew what I was going through, trying to come down. I was getting short, too. The medal had finally come. So really, I was over the peak.

Finally that day came! I was really up as it got nearer and nearer—five, four, three, two. My adrenalin was really going, super happy. The officers teased me about it. "Oh, there's our short-timer. You're not going to be around too much longer, huh, Goff?" "That's right, I'm going stateside, no doubt about it."

I got my orders to Fort Ord, California. I felt pretty good about that since it put me near San Francisco.

The day I see that Big Bird—that was all I had on my mind now. And when I saw that big plane and got on it, boy, I don't know. The feeling that you get on that plane is something that I can't really describe, like you were light as a feather. You were actually high, a feeling that you really cannot explain to anybody. You were in one piece, and you were going to fly that great big bird home.

As the plane went down that landing strip, I looked back and thought of all the guys who were still there. I said a silent prayer for them; and I said a prayer for Bob. "Lord, please have him get out of the boonies; please, please, have him get back to the states." I said that over and over again. We were airborne, and as I looked around and saw how Cam Ranh Bay was jumping into the background, slowly getting smaller and smaller and smaller—I cursed that God damn Vietnam. You know! I said, "May I never have to come back to this bastard. They ain't never getting me to come back here." Vietnam slowly drifted out of sight.

16 STATESIDE

As I [Stan] saw San Francisco come into view, I got excited all over again. The first thing I did when I got off the plane was call my cousins. They were tremendously excited that I was back in the states; I was in one piece, I was OK. They'd heard about me, "You need anybody to pick you up?" "Yeah, I would." They were all out there like a shot. They all hugged and kissed me, "Oh, I heard about you, that was magnificent . . ." I went over to their house. They brought out the bottle. My mother and my girlfriend didn't even know I was back until after they'd called them, because I ended up getting drunk there. I was trying to tell them everything at once and they were asking me everything at once; pretty soon I'd drunk myself into a stupor.

They knew it and carted me off to bed. I slept there for about eight or nine hours, I guess. I woke up and they were still partying. I got back up and we started partying again. Pretty soon my girlfriend came over and picked me up. I went over to her house. I didn't leave there till the next day at four or five o'clock for my mother's house. I'd been back two days and I finally got to her house. It was just one big happy party. When I got to her house, she brought out the bottle. Seems like for days we just celebrated. Wherever I went some guy would want to buy me a drink. It was a great feeling, just that it was all friends. The war was unpopular, but still, I probably should have been given a hero's welcome. There should have been an article in the paper, "DSC Winner Comes Home." But none of this happened.

At that particular time I didn't know what I know now. I was just taking the accolades from my family and personal friends. And that was enough for me at that time. Or I thought it was. People who obviously know better knew that was nothing. Regardless of whether the war was unpopular or not, I was still a DSC winner. I'd seen guys that had Silver Stars get big write-ups in the paper. A Silver Star is a great recognition, don't get me wrong. Those guys deserved their recognition. No press reporter, no television reporter, no radio commentator called me, not even a black radio commentator called and said, "Hey . . ." So, I dunno. After that, I felt that I just wasn't going to get the recognition because I was black.

I got to Fort Ord to start my duty with other Vietnam return-ees who had chips a mile high, "What's happening, man? Hey, what's going on?" Piper was in my unit. I was really happy to see him. He'd been at Ord for a while and was about to get out. Piper was the only guy in my unit that I knew in the Nam. I still had a whole year. We learned that we had to go through regular training bullshit that we had gone through in basic. Some of the guys had been to Germany, but the majority were in the Nam. We had to go out on training routines when we could be training somebody else. I stayed in that unit, went through this bullshit, running every day, and going to these classes with stuff I already knew and already been through. It was called Advanced Technological Training. We were proven GIs, supposedly. The name of the company was Experi-mental Weapons Company. We had to go on maneuvers all the time.

We went out to a place called Hunter Leggett, a place I learned to hate. We'd go all the way down there with everybody moaning and groaning, taking advantage of the fact that we were Vietnam veterans. One day the sergeant major sent out an order that battalion football was about to get started. When I found out that the guys that ended up on the battalion team wouldn't have to pull any duty, I said, "Shit, I'm going out for this right now!" I had my behind out there trying out just like everybody else and made the team as a starter. I said, "All right!" So my ego was about as big as a house. I started playing football for the battalion. I lucked out and had the life of Riley; I didn't have to do shit. All I had to do was make practice and then go back to the barracks and crash; just sensational. I played football for two or three months and then got hurt. One day I was out there hitting like hell, really feeling fierce. I was knocking guys out of the way and running over guys. This one time I ran through the line. There was a little guy who must have been about 110 pounds soaking wet. That little fucker threw a cross body block on me. When we collided, I knocked the shit out of him, but my knees locked; the pain just shot up through my knees.

It was ironic. I went all through the Nam, ending up with a DSC, and then landed in the hospital for major surgery on my knee on account of a football injury.

My entire duty for my last six months was at the hospital. I ETSd out of the army in January of 1970. I never really went back to my unit; I had three days to go before I left Fort Ord. I didn't want to think about how I got myself into this mess after all I went through in the Nam.

When I [Bob] got back to the states, I was supposed to go down to Fort Bragg in North Carolina to my new duty station. By then I suppose I'd had enough of being a paratrooper. If I made it through the Nam, I didn't want to jump no more. Not that I was afraid; not that I wasn't proud of my unit—it was one of the best fighting units in the Nam. I was proud of being a paratrooper, but I had done enough. I put in a request to terminate jump status. I didn't want to go down to Bragg; I wanted to stay in the San Francisco Bay Area. I still had six months to do, so I put in a transfer request and went through more changes. I had to wait in Washington for orders which never came through. Finally, I just took off for San Francisco. My wife was down in Louisiana visiting her parents. I tried to get her to come out to San Francisco and meet me there. I went down to American Airlines, where I'd worked before going to Vietnam, and they gave me a little pass to fly down to Dallas, Texas. I paid my way from there on down to Baton Rouge. I hooked up with my wife. Coming from the Nam, I had a twenty-seven-day leave. Just as I came on the scene there was a new regulation called the 150-day early out, which dropped five months off your service. I missed that by a couple of months. Since I knew my partner, Stan, was down at Fort Ord, I wrote to the Inspector General's Office and got a reply. I immediately flew back to California and went directly to talk to the IG at Fort Ord. There was no parade waiting, no welcome-home-Johnny-glad-you-made-it type of thing.

I called Stan at Fort Ord and told him I was coming down. When I walked into the hospital, the bum was laying up there, eating good chow, having people wait on him like maid service. But Stan is my partner; I love that brother. I thought I was happy when I first got back from Nam, but seeing Stan there was unreal. I had told him I was coming down on Friday, but I walked in on Tuesday and surprised him. He had a cast on at the time, but he almost jumped clean out of bed when he saw me. We had separated a long time ago. It was only a year or so, but it seemed like it had been twenty years since I'd seen him. There he was, with that big smile. We went through the rituals, hugging and hollering, with everybody else on the ward looking; it was great. He had a few friends there. The nurses tried to quiet us down, but to no avail. We were just rejoicing. We talked about what had happened to him over there and what had happened to me and how we got separated when I went to airborne. We talked about that day we split and the empty feeling inside of me that day we separated. We had been partners going all the way back to basic and AIT. We always marched and did calisthenics right next to each other.

Stan got out of the army from the hospital. I finally got an assignment to the reception center at Fort Ord to finish my term. We were separated while he was recuperating because I had to push troops. Since my grandmother was living four blocks from Stan's mother, after he got out of the army, we stayed in contact all the time. In fact, I came home on leave every two weeks.

I was glad to get out and get home. I just caught the Greyhound for San Francisco. When I finally got out, me and my old lady broke up. Then Stan and me were closer than ever. He was sympathizing with the fact that I went through all those changes to keep my woman, and all of a sudden, I lost her when I came out of the war. So we hooked up and just tried to make up the fun part of the life that we had missed. We kicked around, going to bars and listening to live bands. But we never did make up for lost time.

We didn't talk about our feelings that much. But I'll never forget my feeling when I saw Stan that day in the hospital. It was one of the greatest moments in my life, just to realize that we'd survived.

BUNKER HILL

COMMUNITY COLLEGE
CHARLESTOWN, MASS.